By Natsuki Takaya

Tsubasa: Those with Wings Volume 1
Story and Art by Natsuki Takaya

Translation - Kinami Watabe
English Adaptation - Stephanie Duchin
Retouch and Lettering - Star Print Brokers
Production Artist - Michael Paolilli
Graphic Designer - Louis Csontos

Editor - Alexis Kirsch
Pre-Production Supervisor - Vicente Rivera, Jr.
Pre-Production Specialist - Lucas Rivera
Managing Editor - Vy Nguyen
Senior Designer - Louis Csontos
Senior Designer - James Lee
Senior Editor - Bryce P. Coleman
Senior Editor - Jenna Winterberg
Associate Publisher - Marco F. Pavia
President and C.O.O. - John Parker
C.E.O. and Chief Creative Officer - Stu Levy

A TOKYOPOP® Manga

TOKYOPOP Inc.
5900 Wilshire Blvd. Suite 2000
Los Angeles, CA 90036

E-mail: info@TOKYOPOP.com
Come visit us online at www.TOKYOPOP.com

ISBN: 978-1-4278-1428-9

First TOKYOPOP printing: March 2009
10 9 8 7 6 5 4 3 2 1
Printed in the USA

CONTENTS

ヂー

翼(つばさ)を持(も)つ者(もの)
Tsubasa: Those With Wings

Ah, hello...
WELCOME TO OUR STORY OF A WORLD OF LOVE AND LUST.
NOOOO!
IT'S A LIE! HE'S A BIG FAT LIAR!!
Anyhow, here we go...

THERE WERE SO MANY WARS...
THE FIELDS ARE WITHERED AND BUILDINGS LAY IN RUIN.
THE ONLY ONES WHO HAVE ACCESS TO THE NICER AMENITIES NOW ARE THE RICH, THE ARMY, AND THE POLITICIANS.
MEANWHILE, ORDINARY PEOPLE SUFFER IN POVERTY.
THE EARTH IS IN A STATE OF DESOLATION.
WE ARE IN THE 22ND CENTURY.
THIEF!!

WHOA.
IT'S THE THIEF KOTOBUKI!
THUD
Ow.
Damn!!
SHE'S A MONKEY!!
JUMPING AROUND, AS USUAL.
YOU GO AROUND THE BACK--
WHERE'S THE CAPTAIN?!
HE'S GOING SOLO AGAIN.
DAMMIT!
I HATE IT WHEN THEY CALL ME A MONKEY!
GYAAAAH!!
...

KOTOBUKI?
......
RAAAIMON...
MY BAD. YOU OKAY?
IT'S BEEN SIX MONTHS, I THINK.
YOU STEAL ANYTHING GOOD?
Go away!!
YOU'RE AN OFFICER IN THE ARMY!
DON'T YOU HAVE WORK TO DO?!
IF I FELT LIKE IT...
...I COULD CATCH YOU IN A MATTER OF SECONDS.
BUT YOU'RE NOT REALLY WORTH IT.
YOU NEVER STEAL ANYTHING OF VALUE.
ALL YOU DO IS JUMP AROUND LIKE A LITTLE MONKEY.
THAT'S SO MEAN...

SO IT'S BEEN TWO AND A HALF YEARS...
...AND YOU NEVER ARRESTED ME BE-CAUSE...?
I'M DOING YOU A FAVOR.
BASTARD!!
Oh, yeah?
GEE, THANKS!
HE MAKES ME SO MAD.
HE'S IRRESPONSIBLE AND MEAN AS EVER!!
I BET IT WON'T BE LONG BEFORE THEY GET TIRED OF YOU BEING A LOSER!!
......
YOU REALLY WANT TO BET ON THAT?
EH?!
AND IF YOU LOSE...
I'LL GET YOU NEXT TIME.
RUN FOR YOUR LIFE.

No way, Raimon! I'll never take that bet!
Oh!
YOU SCARED ME, KOTOBUKI.
ONE MINUTE YOU'RE SOUND ASLEEP, AND THE NEXT--
OH...
Geez...
I HAD A BAD DREAM...
...ABOUT SOMETHING THAT HAPPENED THREE MONTHS AGO...
RIGHT... IT WAS ONLY THREE MONTHS AGO.
WE SHOULD GET GOING. BREAK TIME IS ALMOST OVER.
AWW...
I'VE MADE A LIVING AS A THIEF SINCE I WAS SIX.
I DID WHAT I HAD TO DO TO SURVIVE.
I HAD NO MONEY, NO PLACE TO STAY.
MY LIFE WAS QUITE MISERABLE.
B-but...!

I FOUND MY FIRST JOB IN THIS TOWN...
Kotobuki?
FIN-ALLY...
I'VE BEEN WAITING FOR THIS DAY FOR 16 YEARS...!!
ON THE DOUBLE, KOTOBUKI!!
HURRY UP AND BRING IN SOME FIREWOOD!!
I GOT IT, OKAY?!!
THE BOSS IS MEAN AND THE WORK IS HARD, BUT...
KOTOBUKI, GO GET PLATES FROM THE BACK.
AND THE ROOF NEEDS REPAIRING!!
Huff
Huff
GOT IT.
HE'S GOING TO BOSS YOU AROUND...
...UNTIL YOU DROP, KOTOBUKI.
It's fine!
IT'S MY JOB TO DO ALL THAT.
IT FEELS A LOT BETTER THAN ROBBING PEOPLE.

AND I'M FAR AWAY FROM RAIMON.
Heh...
HE'D NEVER COME THIS FAR OUT.
HOLD ON A SEC! I DIDN'T RUN AWAY FROM HIM!!
I'M A WANDERER! MY JOURNEY JUST TOOK ME TO THIS TOWN!
WHERE'S MY FOOD, YOU SLACKER?!
WHOA!
OUCH!
WATCH YOUR HAND, OLD MAN!
I almost broke some plates!!
WHO DO YOU THINK YOU'RE TALKING TO?
KOTOBUKI!!!
...I'M SORRY ABOUT THAT...
Tsk!
YOU'D BETTER BE, YOU SCUM!
GEEZ. HE THINKS THAT JUST BECAUSE HE'S THE WEALTHIEST MAN IN TOWN, HE HAS THE RIGHT TO TREAT US LIKE DIRT.
I CAN TAKE CARE OF THE PLATES, KOTOBUKI.
KOTOBUKI?
THANKS.

THE THIEF KOTOBUKI?
ぱしっ
?!
OOF.
...I'LL TAKE THAT AS A YES.
MY NAME IS SHOKA. IT'S NICE TO MEET YOU.
RELAX. WE'RE COL- LEAGUES.
MAY I HAVE A WORD WITH YOU?
WHY ARE YOU WORKING AS A WAITRESS, KOTOBUKI?
...IT'S JUST THAT ROBBING IS NOT MY CALLING.
ANYWAY, WHAT DO YOU WANT?!

I'VE HEARD ABOUT YOU.
A GIRL AROUND 15 OR 16, WHO IS VERY NIMBLE...
...LIKE A MONKEY.
WHY DO THEY ALWAYS SAY THAT?!
Damn!!
YOU'RE NOT MUCH OF A THIEF, BUT YOU'VE GOT SPEED. AND THAT'S A GREAT ASSET.
WHY DON'T YOU COME JOIN US? DON'T GET STUCK HERE.
HELP US FIND TSUBASA.
TSUBASA... YOU MEAN THE TSUBASA?
THAT'S RIGHT. THE LEGENDARY TSUBASA.
YOU'RE ACTUALLY LOOKING FOR IT?
WELL, WE'RE NOT THE ONLY ONES. THERE'RE LOTS OF PEOPLE OUT THERE LOOKING FOR IT.
RUMOR HAS IT THAT THE ARMY'S SECRETLY AFTER IT, TOO.
THERE'S A MYTH...
ONCE UPON A TIME, THERE WAS A SMALL, POOR TOWN.
AND ONE DAY, FROM BELOW THE GROUND...

...TSUBASA EMERGED, SHOOTING OFF THOUSANDS OF LIGHTS...
...AND IT VANISHED AFTER GRANTING EACH OF THE VILLAGERS' WISHES.
SOME BECAME RICH, WHILE SOME GAINED ETERNAL LIFE.
WHAT IT LOOKS LIKE, HOW ONE MAKES IT APPEAR, OR WHY IT IS CALLED TSUBASA REMAINS A MYSTERY, BUT...
SOME PEOPLE BELIEVE THAT IT STILL LAYS SOMEWHERE DEEP IN THE GROUND, AND THAT WHOEVER FINDS IT...
...WILL GET HIS WISH...
I'VE GOT A JOB, SO I'M NOT INTERESTED.
...SORRY ABOUT THAT.
YOU CAN DROP THE TOUGH GIRL ACT, YOU STUPID CHILD.
Well, damn.
GRR...
WHAT DID YOU SAY?!!
YOU BETTER NOT UNDERPLAY OUR BOSS.
SEE YOU LATER.
THIS ISN'T OVER. YOU HAVEN'T SEEN THE LAST OF US, HONEY.

SHE CAN BE A REAL BITCH, AND SHE CAN'T RUN AND HAS TERRIBLE AIM.
DON'T SAY ANOTHER WORD!!
I'll hit you!!
UH, OKAY...
I NEVER THOUGHT THAT SOME PEOPLE ACTUALLY BELIEVED IN IT...
"DROP THE TOUGH GIRL ACT."
HOW DARE SHE!
I'VE ALWAYS BEEN ON MY OWN.
EVERY DAY, I'VE BEEN THE ONLY ONE I COULD RELY ON...
...BECAUSE THERE WAS NO ONE TO TURN TO.
カン
カン
コン
カーン
TSU-BASA...
TSUBASA GRANTS EVERYONE'S WISHES...
ボワン
Shit.
BOSS?!
I'M ON IT, SIR...
GO AWAY. I DON'T WANT YOU!!
ぶんぶんぶんぶ
STOP IT. I'VE GOT WORK TO DO!!
KOTOBUKI.
....
ポロ

R--
UH.
RAIMON?!
HEY.
LONG TIME NO SEE.
HE'S REAL!!
BUT... WHY?
Y-YOU...
WHAT'RE YOU DOING...?
WHAT AM I SAYING?!
I'M ON VACATION.
B-BUT WHY ARE YOU OUT IN THE MIDDLE OF NOWHERE...?!
KOTOBUKI.

I DIDN'T KNOW YOU WORE A GIRDLE. THAT'S FRAUD.
What are you, crazy?!!
SO I GOT A GLIMPSE.
YOU COULD'VE CLOSED YOUR EYES!!
GASP!
UH, ABOUT THAT BET...
DID...
DID YOU REALLY MEAN IT...?
BET?
WHAT BET?
...RIGHT.
Heh...
I KNEW IT.
I SHOULDN'T HAVE TAKEN YOU SERIOUSLY, BUT...

You really forgot about it?!
YOUR IRRESPON-SIBILITY KNOWS NO BOUNDS!!
I'VE BEEN BUSY...
GOOD GIRL.
ポン
ポン
FORGET IT!!
I DON'T WANT ANYTHING TO DO WITH THE ARMY!!
YOU WORKING HERE?
WELL...
IT'S NOTHING BIG, BUT--
WAIT.
How do you know...?
BRING ME MY BREAKFAST, WILL YOU?
YOU'RE ACTUALLY STAYING HERE?!
WELL, GREAT.
I WAS SO MAD, I COULDN'T SLEEP.
I NEVER EXPECTED TO SEE HIM HERE...
KOTO-BUKI.
Morning grocery shopping

THAT RAIMON GUY THAT'S STAYING HERE. IS HE IN THE ARMY?
HOW DID YOU KNOW?!
I OVERHEARD THE TWO OF YOU YELLING YESTERDAY. YOU KNOW EACH OTHER?
WELL, A BIT...
I'M SO GLAD I DIDN'T SAY ANYTHING ABOUT BEING A THIEF...
GOOD FOR YOU. KNOWING SOMEONE FROM THE ARMY.
I'VE SEEN SOME OFFICERS IN TOWN, BUT THEY ALL LOOK SCARY.
Is that so?
THAT'S THEIR JOB, AFTER ALL. RAIMON'S AN EXCEPTION...
DO YOU THINK HE'S ONE OF THE ARMY'S ELITE?
I HEARD THAT IF YOU WORK YOUR WAY UP TO CAPTAIN, YOU'RE REWARDED WITH A HOUSE WITH ELECTRICITY AND RUNNING WATER!!
YOU KNOW, THAT RAIMON IS SO COOL! ♡ COULD YOU ASK IF HE HAS A GIRLFRIEND?
No...
NOT A CHANCE!!
Money and glory... The elite have it all.
Oh?
WHY NOT?
WELL...

BECAUSE...
......
HE MIGHT GET A FUNNY IDEA.
YOU KNOW!!
Wait... KOTOBUKI?
HE'S BEEN LIKE THAT EVER SINCE WE MET.
HE'S AN IRRESPONSIBLE AND MANIPULATIVE JERK.
ふははは
はは
HE THINKS IT'S ALL A BIG JOKE!!
"NICE TO MEET YOU."
"ARE YOU KOTOBUKI? YOU'RE CUTE."
"AND YOU'RE AN IDIOT. DO YOUR JOB."
"I WILL..."
"...EVENTUALLY."
THAT'S RIGHT. WHY WOULD I WANT TO ASK HIM THAT?
Ha!
WHAT A JOKE.
HE'D THINK I WAS INTERESTED IN HIM!!
THAT'D BE DIS-GUSTING!
KYAA!!

HUH...?
A LETTER?
Old-fashioned--
ARE YOU GOING TO READ IT...?
Careful...
..."KOTOBUKI IS BAD NEWS. FIRE HER OR SOMETHING BAD WILL HAPPEN..."
WH--
THAT'S AWFUL.
...TOOOOBUUUKI!!!??
Boss
GAH!
IT MUST BE THAT WOMAN...
SHOKA!!
KO...
How im-mature.
What have you done this time?!
Explain! Now!
......
Wait--
HOLD ON A SEC, BOSS!!

Shut up!!
HOW MUCH DO YOU THINK GLASS COSTS NOWADAYS?
DEDUCT IT FROM MY SALARY!!
JUST DON'T DO THIS TO ME!!
I DON'T WANT ANY TROUBLE. BEAT IT!!
AH!
HOLD ON A SEC! YOU HAVEN'T PAID ME YET!
A-AND I DIDN'T GET TO EAT MY BREAKFAST, AND...
SHUT UP AND LEAVE!
DAMN...
NOT AGAIN...
ALL I WANTED WAS TO START A NEW, CLEAN LIFE.
I WORKED SO HARD FOR IT...
BUT I SUPPOSE...
...I HAD IT COMING.
THIS...
...IS ONE OF THOSE TIMES...
...WHEN I FEEL LIKE...
...I COULD REALLY USE A BIG SHOULDER TO LEAN ON.

Grrr...
Again
FORGET THAT! SULKING WON'T GET ME ANYWHERE!!
THEY CAN'T GET ME DOWN!!
Why did I have to think of him?!
I GUESS IT'S BACK TO A LIFE OF...
... CRIME.
HOW-EVER...
...I'M SO HUNGRY ...
What?!
IS THAT TRUE, SIR?!!
KEEP YOUR VOICE DOWN, YOU IMBECILE!!
!
THAT'S THE RICH GUY FROM YESTER-DAY...
ANYWAY.
THIS IS EXTREMELY VALUABLE.

WHAT'S THAT?
IT'S SOMETHING THE ARMY WOULD KILL TO HAVE.
I CAN'T WAIT TO FIND OUT HOW MUCH THEY'RE WILLING TO PAY FOR IT.
IT'S THE ONLY ONE IN THE WORLD.
WHAT ARE THEY TALKING ABOUT?
"...THE ARMY'S SECRETLY AFTER IT, TOO."
Oh!
COULD BE...
...TSUBASA...?
HM...?
ブルルルルル
......!!
NOT SO LOUD.
NGHHH! NGHHH!
I HEAR YOU GOT FIRED.
ひしっ
YOU POOR THING...
Get off!
Oh.

LISTEN, I'M BACK IN THE GAME AS OF TODAY!!
I CAN'T GET COMFY WITH AN OFFICER!
THEN YOU NEED TO BE A NOTCH UP FROM THAT.
How's that?!
I AM A NOTCH UP!
DO YOU EVEN GET THE MEANING OF THAT PHRASE?
IT'LL BE FINE. I CAN FIND ANOTHER JOB. UNTIL THEN...
...I'LL JUST GET BETTER AT STEALING--
YOU'RE SHAKING.
ARE YOU AFRAID?
I...
LET GO OF ME, YOU LOSER!!
ANYWAY, I'M GOING TO--
BREAK IN THAT MAN'S HOUSE?
UH.
How'd you know?!
It's obvious.
I DIDN'T KNOW YOU WERE INTERESTED IN TSUBASA--
I-I--
I'M JUST CURIOUS...
That's all...

I'M GOING WITH YOU.
WHA--?
YOU WORK FOR THE LAW ENFORCEMENT, REMEMBER?!
I'M ON VACATION.
Idiot!!
THAT DOESN'T MAKE IT OKAY!!
I WON'T STEAL ANYTHING.
I'LL JUST WATCH.
HAVE YOU NO PRIDE AS AN OFFICER?!
?
?!
Oh.
HE'S THE OFFICER IN CHARGE OF THIS SECTOR.
POOR CAPTAIN YUGEN, WASTING AWAY IN THE COUNTRYSIDE.
City dweller
CRUD!
Let's get going.
WE'VE GOT TO GO.
Wait.
WHY ARE YOU FOLLOWING ME?
YOU KNOW WHY.

ギュッ
I JUST WANT TO BE WITH YOU, KOTOBUKI.
......
AND...
SOON ENOUGH YOU'LL FORGET WHAT YOU JUST SAID, JUST LIKE YOU DID WITH THE BET.
WHAT DO YOU WANT FROM ME? ARE YOU PULLING MY LEG?
I CAN'T ASK THAT, THOUGH.
WHEN DID HE START HAVING THIS EFFECT ON ME?
I'M DANCING TO HIS RHYTHM.
I WISH I KNEW HOW HE FEELS ABOUT ME.
IF ONLY I HAD TSUBASA...
...TSUBASA COULD MAKE THAT HAPPEN.
IF I HAD TSUBASA, I WOULD BE ABLE TO TELL.

BOSS.
KOTOBUKI IS ON THE MOVE.
GOT IT.
LOOKS LIKE OUR LETTER WORKED.
LET'S FOLLOW HER UNTIL SHE GIVES IN AND JOINS US.
SHE'S GOT COMPANY. A GUY...
THEN TAKE CARE OF HIM.
Let's go!!
DOES SHE EVER WORK...?
DON'T EVEN BOTHER, OR SHE'LL START CHUCKING EXPLOSIVES AT YOU.
She always misses, though.
...SO THIS IS HIS HOUSE.
Okay...
SO HOW ARE WE GOING TO GET IN?
YOU'RE REALLY COMING ALONG?!

YOU WANT A QUICK MEAL?
CAN I COME WITH YOU?
"CAN" I?
CAN I?
DO WHAT YOU WANT!!
Yay!
......
OKAY! LET'S GO.
すく

DO YOU MIND IF I GO FIRST?
IF I GO DOWN FROM HERE--
"I DIDN'T KNOW YOU WORE A GIRDLE. THAT'S FRAUD."
BLUSH
NO!! I'LL GO FIRST!!
Final word!!
...OKAY...
MAYBE ...
...I SHOULD'VE CHANGED MY CLOTHES...
I DON'T KNOW WHERE TO START...
WHAT'RE YOU DOING?
Gaaah!
AH.
I THINK WE'VE FOUND SOME-THING.
HM?

WHAT ARE THOSE?
PROOF THAT HE GOT WEALTHY BY BUYING AND SELLING ILLEGAL STUFF.
I SEE.
Look!
HE'S ALSO EVADING HIS TAXES.
バサ
バサ
WHAT AM I DOING?! I'M NOT HERE FOR THAT!!
バサ
KOTO-BUKI?
BUSTED...
...
WHY CAN'T I...
WHAT THE HELL?!
!
WHAT DO YOU WANT?!
WHAT ARE YOU DOING?!
...DO ONE THING...
...WITHOUT MESSING UP...?
YOU KNOW YOU NEED A PERMIT TO OWN A GUN.
Issued by the Army.

BUT YOU GOT IT ILLEGALLY, DIDN'T YOU?
Naughty old man.
Shut up!!
YOU'VE SEEN TOO MUCH. I'M AFRAID I'LL HAVE TO KILL BOTH OF YOU.
Aren't you scared?
GIVE US A SEND-OFF GIFT.
WHERE DID YOU STASH "THE ONLY ONE IN THE WORLD"?
Ah.
SO THAT'S WHAT YOU WERE LOOKING FOR.
IT'S NOT HERE. I HID IT IN A SAFE PLACE.
LIKE...
...THE PLACE WHERE YOU HOLD AUCTIONS?
Ack!
YOU SHOULD WATCH THAT BIG MOUTH OF YOURS.
YOU'RE TOO DUMB TO MAKE GOOD USE OF IT.
Hey, don't provoke him. He's got a gun...
You little--
YOU ARE NOT GOING TO TAKE ANYTHING FROM ME.
NOT A PENNY. NOT A THING.
THEY'RE ALL MINE!
HE SAID HE'S GOT CLUES ON TSUBASA IN THIS HOUSE!!
?!

WHERE?!
WHERE IS IT?!
YOU KNEW SHE WAS FOLLOWING US, DIDN'T YOU?!
YEP.
Whaaaat?!
HE'S OUT COLD.
WHERE IS IT, KOTO--
HE'S USELESS, THEN.
Damn...
GAH!!
Ra-
RAIMON?!
ずざっ
YOU TWO KNOW EACH OTHER?!
You...
YEP.
WHAT ARE YOU DOING HERE?
YOU QUIT THE ARMY...
...TWO MONTHS AGO!!

......
Heh.
WHAT'RE YOU TALKING ABOUT? HE'S ON VACATION.
NO, WHAT ARE YOU TALKING ABOUT?!
I KNOW BECAUSE I WAS THERE!!
"I'M GOING TO LET YOU ESCAPE."
"THEY CAN BLAME ME, AND IT'LL MAKE IT EASIER FOR ME TO QUIT THE ARMY."
"YOU'RE GOING TO ABANDON YOUR STATUS?!"
"THERE IS SOMETHING I WANT TO DO."
AND JUST LIKE THAT, HE QUIT!!
IS THAT TRUE...?
YEAH.
WHY...
...DID HE LIE?
IS THAT WHY...
...YOU NEVER ARRESTED ME?
BECAUSE THERE WAS SOMETHING ELSE YOU'D RATHER DO...?
"I'LL GET YOU NEXT TIME."

SO THE BET REALLY WAS JUST A WHIM OF YOURS.
AND YOU FORGOT ALL ABOUT IT.
ANYWAY, I AM EXTREMELY CLOSE TO GETTING TSUBASA.
I'm not afraid of Raimon!
LOOKS LIKE I DON'T NEED YOUR HELP AFTER ALL, KOTOBUKI...
HEY!!
I was still talking!!
TSUBASA...
...IS MINE!
BOM
BOM
WHOA!
THIS IS TOO MUCH, EVEN FOR TSUBASA.
OUCH...
I've got dirt in my eye...
GEEZ. SHE'S HORRIBLE.
WHAT SHOULD I DO?
HELP ME, TSUBASA.
GYAAA!
RAIMON...?
WHERE...?

!!
JUST GREAT... YOU ALMOST HAD ME FOOLED, KOTOBUKI.
カッ
カッ
YOU WANT TSUBASA, TOO, DON'T YOU?
THERE'S NOTHING WRONG WITH THAT. TSUBASA CAN MAKE YOU RICH. NO MORE ROBBING, RIGHT?
IT OPENS DOORS TO EVERYTHING.
YOU DON'T EVEN HAVE TO WORK FOR IT!
DEEP DOWN, EVERYBODY WANTS AN EASY LIFE.
I DON'T KNOW WHAT YOU WERE DOING WORKING STEADY...
...BUT YOU'RE NO DIFFERENT THAN THE OTHERS.
...MAYBE SHE'S RIGHT.
MAYBE IT WAS POINTLESS TO EVEN TRY.
Wow, boss!! You're a bitch!!
Shut it!!
I JUST DIDN'T WANT TO ADMIT IT.
IF I LOST FAITH IN MYSELF, I WOULDN'T BE ABLE TO KEEP GOING.
SHE'S RIGHT.

I WAS JUST ACTING TOUGH.
NOT ME.
IF I REALLY WANTED SOMETHING...
...I'D WANT TO EARN IT ON MY OWN.
LET'S GO.
......
THEN MIND YOUR OWN BUSINESS!!
STOP MESSING WITH KOTOBUKI.
YOU--
げしっ
HANG IN THERE, BOSS!!
You look really stupid!!

OW!
OH.
WHAT WAS THAT NOISE?!
THE POLICE!!
CAPTAIN RAIMON?!
IS THAT CAPTAIN RAIMON SHIRAGI?!
......
THIS IS WHERE HE HIDES HIS STASH.
HUH?
IF YOU DON'T WANT TO GET CAUGHT...
...GO ON WITHOUT ME WHILE I TALK TO HIM.
OH... OKAY.
LONG TIME NO SEE, YUGEN.
IT IS GOOD TO SEE YOU.
WE'VE BEEN LOOKING FOR YOU.
PLEASE GET IN THE CAR!!
HUH?
WAIT.
WHAT'S GOING...
...ON?

THERE'S NO WAY THEY'RE TAKING HIM BACK...
IS THERE?
BUT...
TSUBASA CAN GET YOU ANYTHING...
YOU DON'T EVEN HAVE TO WORK FOR IT!
"NOT ME."
"IF I WANTED SOMETHING..."
"I'D WANT TO EARN IT ON MY OWN."
"GOOD GIRL."

RAIMON!!
WAIT UP!!
WHO'S THAT BRAT? WHAT DOES SHE WANT WITH CAPTAIN SHIRAGI?
And she's on a first-name basis?!
I'M NO GOOD.
I CAN'T DO ANYTHING RIGHT.
BUT... I'VE BEEN TRYING.
Wha?
SO...
I HAVE TO ASK HIM WHAT HE REALLY WANTS.
Ack!
I NEED TO FIND OUT FOR MYSELF.

I'VE GOT TO GO FOR IT!!
STAY WHERE YOU ARE!!
EVERYONE HAS HIGH HOPES FOR YOU, RAIMON.
THEY MADE YOU A CAPTAIN AS PART OF THE TRAINING.
YOU HAVE A GREAT CAREER AHEAD OF YOU.
COME BACK WITH US.
!?
RAIMON? WHAT--
DIDN'T I TELL YOU?
THERE IS SOMETHING ELSE I WANT TO DO.
MIND IF I BORROW THIS?
RAIMON--
WHOA!
LATER!

Huff
Huff
BUT...
Huff
Huff
Huff
I BET...
Huff
Huff
...SHOKA DOESN'T UNDERSTAND WHAT I'M...
...DOING...
Huff
Huff
IF YOU EARN IT ON YOUR OWN...
...WHAT YOU GET IS MUCH MORE MEANINGFUL.
RA...
HOP ON.
WHA?!
RAIMON SHIRAGI...
...I DON'T UNDER-STAND YOU.
Ahhh!
WHAT IS IT YOU REALLY WANT?

DON'T WORRY.
I WAS COMING BACK TO YOU!
......
RAIMON, I...
HOLD ON TIGHT.
HUH?
Whaaat?!
WHA ?!
EXCUSE ME.
Ahhh!!
※Hot
WAI--
STOP--
GAH!

…ん
ハッ
WE'RE HERE.
ドルン
I, UH, KIND OF WRECKED THAT, DIDN'T I?
ドルン
ギッ
ドルン
YOU IDIOT!!
FIST
Head
YOU COULD'VE GOTTEN US KILLED!!
YOU'RE ALWAYS JERKING ME AROUND...
...YOU RECKLESS BASTARD...!
I DON'T REGRET IT.
......
I DON'T.
I WAS JUST AFRAID...
...OF FINDING OUT THAT HE WAS JUST IN IT, TO HAVE SOME FUN.
I'D BE LOST, IF THAT WERE TRUE.

I COULDN'T SHOW MY FEAR, THOUGH...
...SINCE IT WAS TIME TO FIND OUT THE TRUTH.
OTHERWISE I'D DIE OF RAIMON DISEASE.
KOTOBUKI.
YOU'RE CUTE.
!!
...WH--
WHY...?
OH, DON'T CRY.
IT ONLY MAKES ME WANT TO TEASE YOU MORE.
WHY ARE YOU DOING THIS TO ME?

YOU CAN HATE ME ALL YOU WANT. I'D UNDERSTAND.
I'VE LIED TO YOU AND JERKED YOU AROUND...
I TOLD YOU.
...JUST TO GET YOUR ATTEN-TION.
SORRY, BUT THAT'S ME.
I'LL NEVER LET YOU GO.
"YOU REALLY WANT TO BET ON THAT?"
"I'LL GET YOU NEXT TIME."
"AND IF YOU LOSE..."
I WILL MAKE YOU MINE.

But...
YOU SAID YOU'D FORGOTTEN!!
I DIDN'T SAY THAT.
IS THAT WHAT YOU WANTED TO DO? TO WIN THE BET...?
Th-that's...
BINGO.
YOU LEFT ALL THE GLORY FOR ME?!
YOU CAN'T BE MORE PRECISE.
ALL I WANTED WAS TO END THE WHOLE OFFICER-THIEF THING SO I COULD BE WITH YOU.
S--
STUPID. I'M SO STUPID.
THAT'S...
...WHAT MAKES YOU SO IRRESISTIBLE.
RAIMON...
LOOK BEHIND--

Oh!
THIS IS IT. THIS IS HIS STASH.
IT'S SHORTED OUT.
IS THIS THE CLUE TO TSUBASA?
They're in uniforms. Are they Army?
I DON'T THINK SO. THESE ARE IMAGES OF HUMAN BEINGS BEFORE THE 22ND CENTURY.
WHAT THE...
EH...?
We got it wrong?
THEY CAN BE QUITE VALUABLE, SINCE MOST REFERENCES WERE BURNED DURING THE WARS.
I'M NOT SURE IF TSUBASA REALLY EXISTS ANYMORE...
NOT MY PROBLEM.
BUT MAYBE IT DOESN'T HAVE TO BE BLACK AND WHITE.
YOU SEARCH FOR TSUBASA. YOU DREAM ABOUT IT. YOU INVEST IN IT.

YOU NEED SOMETHING TO LIVE FOR...
...ANY DAY.
...YEAH.
ME...
...TOO.
HUMANS ARE WEAK.
BOOM
どぉ〜ん
!?
Sho...
SHOKA...?!
Please stop that. The building is falling out.
Damn you, Raimon!
SHE'S MAKING THINGS EVEN MORE OF A PROBLEM.
Ahhh!!
THERE'S A HOLE IN THE WALL!!
That's your work, isn't it?!
THE DOOR IS BLOCKED, AND THERE'S SHOKA, NOW, TOO.

WE'LL HAVE TO JUMP OFF.
ARE YOU INSANE? LOOK AT THE HEIGHT!!
I-I can't.
DON'T WORRY. I'M THE LUCKY ONE.
Uwaaa... That is so not comforting!
OH!
ガラ
THERE YOU ARE, RAIMON!!
LET'S GO.
Gaaah!
THINK BEFORE YOU ACT, YOU IDIOT!!
I'm gonna die!
SHOKA'S SPECIAL BOMB!!
Eat this!!
HE'S CRAZY!
WHY DOES IT HAVE TO BE HIM?
WHY? WHY?!
UGHH!!

RIGHT..
ぷはっ
Koff
Koff
OH.
Ouch!!
YOU KNEW THERE WAS A LAKE?!
MAYBE?
HE GOT ME...
I GUESS.
...AGAIN.

YOU JUST WATCH.
Damn!
Ah ha ha ha...
I WILL STEAL YOUR HEART AND NEVER LET YOU GO.
EEK!!
YOU'RE NOT GOING TO LET HER WALK AWAY WITH NOTHING, RIGHT?
AFTER EVERYTHING SHE'S DONE FOR YOU?
I-
I'LL CONSIDER RE-HIRING HER...
So please don't hit me.
Bully...
WHY SHOULD I TRUST HER WITH YOU?
I--
CAPTAIN RAIMON.
SO YOU'RE REALLY NOT COMING BACK?

DON'T YOU KNOW THE OLD SAYING?
HE WHO COMES BETWEEN TWO LOVERS...
...SHALL DIE...
...AFTER BEING KICKED BY A HORSE.
Coming from him, it sounds like a real threat.
WELL, THAT GIRL'S IN FOR A ROUGH RIDE...
...NOW THAT RAIMON'S FOUND HER.
KOTOBUKI.
YOUR BOSS ASKED ME TO HAND THIS TO YOU.
HE'D FORGOTTEN ABOUT IT.
OH?!
WOW!
MY FIRST SALARY.
WOW! WOW!
I FEEL AS IF I CAN DO ANYTHING!
Like finding another job.
I'M LEAVING.
HUH...?
BUT... RAIMON?!

RAI--!!
NOT.
......
THIS GUY IS--!!
I GOT YOU THERE, DIDN'T I?
Dammit!!
GO AHEAD AND LEAVE. SEE IF I CARE.
YOU'RE SO CUTE. YOU KNOW THAT, KOTOBUKI?
Shut up, loser!!
Back to Shoka.
WHERE'S THE CLUE?!
I WANT TO GO HOME.

翼を持つ者

THE END OF THE 22ND CENTURY: EARTH.
PLEASE, HIRE ME!!
Can't.
I CAN'T AFFORD TO HIRE ANYONE IN THESE HARD TIMES.
NOT IN THIS DRIED-UP VILLAGE WHERE CROPS RARELY GROW.
THERE WERE SO MANY WARS...
...THAT HAVE SINCE LEFT THE FIELDS WITHERED. ONLY THE UPPER CLASS PEOPLE, LIKE THE ARMY AND POLITICIANS, ENJOY THE NICER AMENITIES.
LOOK, I CAN CLIMB. I'VE GOT THE SPEED. I'VE GOT THE STRENGTH!!
Look at me!!
Rocks
We just sell household supplies.
SOUNDS LIKE YOU'D MAKE AN EXCELLENT THIEF.
Wh--
WHAT ARE YOU TALKING ABOUT? WHY WOULD I DO THAT?!
I WANT TO WORK!!
I'M KOTOBUKI. I'M A FORMER THIEF WHO'S LOOKING FOR A REAL JOB.
PEOPLE ARE FORCED TO LIVE IN POVERTY. THE STREETS ARE RIFE WITH CRIMINALS.

I USED TO BE A FULL-TIME THIEF. I WAS DOING WHAT I HAD TO DO...
...TO SURVIVE THE HARD TIMES.
キイ…
Bar
HOW COME NOBODY WANTS ME...?
I'VE BEEN TRAVELING FROM TOWN TO TOWN.
ガヤ
ガヤ
ONE MONTH AGO, I GAINED A COMPANION.
THANKS FOR WAITING, RAIMON.
HUH?!
Where'd he go?!
わあ…
AND THAT COMPANION...
...IS HIM.
JUST GREAT.
YOU WIN AGAIN.
RAI... MON?!
Ra-
MAH-JONG. YOU KNOW HIM? HE'S PRETTY DAMN GOOD.
ジャラ
ジャラ
WHAT THE HECK IS HE DOING?!

HE'S CHEATING...
THIS GAME IS RIGGED!
The table ...
THAT IS AN INSULT.
HOW DARE YOU BRING ME DOWN TO YOUR LEVEL?
I'M A GENIUS. THERE'S NO BETTER WORD TO DESCRIBE ME.
Didn't you know that?
RAIMON SHIRAGI: A MEAN AND MANIPULA-TIVE JERK.
I CAN'T BELIEVE HE USED TO BE AN ELITE CAPTAIN IN THE ARMY.
What an odd world.
sigh
YOU MADE A KILLING, BUDDY.
Can I pick your brain?
OH, IT'S YOU, KOTOBUKI.

HOW DID JOB HUNTING GO?
SORRY I KEPT YOU WAITING, BUT CAN'T YOU JUST ACT NORMAL?
HEY, DID YOU HEAR?
THAT MAN WAS SO MEAN. HE CALLED ME A FAKE.
And you're itching for a beating.
THE ARMY IS THE PLACE FOR THE PRIVILEGED FEW.
That man scared me out of my wits.
GET. OFF.
Damn. He's got company.
He's out of it.
WORD HAS IT RAIMON WAS A YOUNG CAPTAIN FAST ON TRACK IN THE FORCE. (THIS MAY SOUND UNBELIEVABLE.)
Tsubasa Memo
The force Raimon belonged to is something like the police.
RAIMON WOULD CHASE AFTER ME IN HIS OWN FUSSY WAY WHEN I WAS A THIEF.
(She's in the middle of a robbery.)
Wanna chocolate, Kotobuki?
ONE DAY HE JUST SHOWED UP AND...
Yo.
AFTER A BIT OF FIGHT WITH A FEMALE THIEF CALLED SHOKA...
What?
Her boys
...I FOUND OUT THAT RAIMON LEFT THE ARMY.
"ALL I WANTED..."

"...WAS TO END THE WHOLE OFFICER-THIEF THING SO I COULD BE WITH YOU."
AND HERE WE ARE.
カァァ
We--
WE KIND OF LOOK LIKE A COUPLE...!
WHAT'S THE MATTER? YOU'RE NOT HUNGRY?
I SUPPOSE YOU HAD NO LUCK JOB HUNTING.
"Suppose" my ass.
WE'RE TRAVELING FROM TOWN TO TOWN LOOKING FOR A JOB.
SO WHY HAVEN'T I HAD ANY LUCK SO FAR?
DON'T WORRY. I'M MAKING MONEY.
No!
No way!!
I'VE GOT A LIST OF THINGS YOU HAVE PAID FOR ME!!
THOSE ARE ALL SELF-IMPOSED DEBTS...

WHY ARE YOU SO UPSET?
Ngh.
COME ON, THERE'RE NO SECRETS BETWEEN US.
Gaaah!!
I WISH THERE WAS A JOB LAYING AROUND FOR ME TO PICK UP!!
ザワ
ザワ
WHAT'S GOING ON?
IT'S SARABINA.
THE SARABINA TSUBASA CULT.
TSUBASA... CULT?
TSUBASA IS A MYTH OF THIS TIME.
ONCE UPON A TIME... TSUBASA EMERGED FROM THE GROUND, SHOOTING OFF LIGHTS.
IT GRANTED EVERY VILLAGER'S WISH AND THEN DISAPPEARED INTO THIN AIR.

NOBODY KNOWS WHAT IT LOOKS LIKE, OR WHERE IT CAME FROM.
BUT SOME PEOPLE BELIEVE THAT TSUBASA IS STILL SOMEWHERE DEEP IN THE GROUND...
...AND THAT WHOEVER FINDS IT WILL BE GRANTED HIS WISH...
AS YOU'RE AWARE...
...THE FIELDS... THE EARTH IS WITHERED.
THE PLANET DOES NOT HAVE THE ABILITY TO EXPRESS HER PAIN LIKE US. SHE HAS TO SUFFER IN SILENCE.
THE DEATH OF THE EARTH... IS THE DEATH OF US.
TSUBASA IS OUR ONLY HOPE.
WE NEED ITS ABSOLUTE POWER TO SAVE THE PLANET.
NOW WE MAY BE POWERLESS ON OUR OWN...
...BUT IF WE STICK TOGETHER AND PRAY FOR THE LOVE OF TSUBASA...
TSUBASA WILL DESCEND ONTO THE EARTH ONCE AGAIN AND SAVE US ALL.
THAT IS OUR PRAYER, SARABINA'S BELIEF.

わあ…
パチ
パチ
パチ
Kotobuki, want another nikuman?
...I'VE HEARD OF SEVERAL TSUBASA CULTS...
...BUT I'VE NEVER HEARD OF SARABINA.
Uh-huh.
OF COURSE YOU HAVEN'T. THE CULT IS ONLY SIX MONTHS OLD. THEY BUILT A TOWER NEAR THE VILLAGE.
IT'S NOT THAT I DON'T BELIEVE IN TSUBASA, BUT...
Cults aren't my thing...
ムグ
ムグ
THAT GUY, DUMA, IS THE HEAD. HE GOES AROUND PREACHING PRETTY MUCH EVERY DAY.
THE WHOLE BUSINESS ABOUT TSUBASA IS BOGUS.
Half the village doesn't believe it.
YOU DON'T LOOK FAMILIAR.
ARE YOU A VISITOR?
OH!
ERM...
IF YOU'RE INTERESTED, YOU ARE ALWAYS WELCOME TO VISIT...
...OUR TOWER.

Editor's note: Nikuman is a steamed meat bun.

WHAT... IS THAT?
THOSE REVOLVING THINGS...
IT'S SARABINA'S SYMBOL TOWER.
YOU HAVE BAD TASTE.
RAIMON!!
MASTER DUMA...
AH. I MUST GO.
LET THE HAND OF TSUBASA TOUCH UPON YOU...
OKAY...
A SYMBOL TOWER... HOW INTER-ESTING.
ザワ
ザワ
PRETTY GUY, BUT THERE'S SOMETHING WEIRD ABOUT HIM...
ザワ

That's right.
DON'T LET THAT SMILE OF HIS FOOL YOU. YOU NEVER KNOW WHAT'S REALLY GOING ON IN HIS HEAD.
Heh.
AND WHY DOES THAT ONLY REMIND ME OF YOU?
SIR... ABOUT THAT MAN. HE WAS BEING CALLED RAIMON...
I HEARD...
WELL, WELL... THIS IS A NICE SURPRISE.
WE HAVE TO PREPARE FOR OUR SPECIAL GUESTS.

SO...
DO YOU WANT TO KEEP LOOKING FOR A JOB HERE, OR ARE WE GOING TO THE NEXT TOWN?
Hmm...
LET'S SEE. PEOPLE HERE SEEM TO BE BARELY FEEDING THEMSELVES...
Camping
OR WE COULD JOIN SARABINA AND PRAY FOR TSUBASA.
DON'T EVEN GO THERE.
WHAT IS IT?
I LIKE TO LOOK AFTER MYSELF...
WHAT'S THAT? ON YOUR CHEST...
THIS? IT'S A TATTOO.
THEY MADE ME GET ONE WHEN I ENTERED THE ARMY.
Right...
THE SIGHT OF IT REMINDS ME THAT YOU WERE AN OFFICER.
SO NO MORE ROBBING? WAS IT A CLEAN BREAK?
GRR
OF COURSE!! WHAT DO YOU MEAN?!
DO YOU HAVE A PROBLEM WITH THAT?

TEMPER, TEMPER.
I DIDN'T MEAN IT THAT WAY, OKAY?
I WILL...
...STILL LOVE YOU NO MATTER WHAT.
ぎくっ
HUH?
BUT DON'T WALK AWAY FROM ME, OKAY?
WAIT--
RA--
N--
No, stop!!
I'M SLEEPY AND IT ACHES, I MEAN, MY HEAD, BECAUSE OF A HEADACHE!!
That was redundant.
WHEN YOU STOP FREAKING OUT OVER A KISS...
...WE'LL BE ABLE TO SHARE A BED.

Keep dreaming, loser!!
GOOD NIGHT.
...AWW.
DAMMIT...
WE'VE BEEN TRAVELING TOGETHER FOR A MONTH.
IT'S LONG ENOUGH FOR ME TO KNOW HIS COMPETENCE.
HE'S CAPABLE AND SMART. THERE'S NOTHING HE CAN'T DO.
WHAT ABOUT ME?
I WAS A THIEF, BUT THAT'S ALL BEHIND ME.
I CAN'T LET RAIMON SEE ME...
...USE STOLEN MONEY. IT'S EMBARRASSING.
DO YOU WANT TO STAY AS A GOOD-FOR-NOTHING?
OF COURSE NOT!!
FIRST THING'S FIRST, I NEED TO FIND SOME WORK...
YEAH, EVERYTHING IS HUNKY-DORY...

KOTOBUKI, WHAT TIME DO YOU WANT TO WAKE UP TOMORROW...?
......
......
GO ROT IN HELL!!
OOPS. SORRY!
Got an eyeful.
Hell...
Hell...
BOSS...
THAT ECHOING VOICE SOUNDED FAMILIAR.
YOU MUST BE IMAGING IT.
LET'S PRETEND WE DIDN'T HEAR IT, RIGHT, BOSS?

JOB, EH? GOT ONE FOR ME, TOO?!
SORRY.
YOU HAVE TO GO SOME-WHERE ELSE.
NOBODY WANTS ME...
I'LL GO CHECK ON RAIMON AGAIN...
くすん
I BET HE'S STILL PLAYING MAH-JONG!
HM?
WHAT'S UP, KIDDO?
Did you drop something?
THERE'RE NO BUDS...
WE WORK ON THE FIELDS EVERY YEAR, BUT THERE'S NO SIGN OF THEM.
MAYBE TSUBASA IS THE ONLY ANSWER...
I HAVE AN IDEA.
Whee!
Yay!

WHAT DO YOU THINK OF THIS SOIL?
Yay!
IT'S WON-DERFUL!
yay!
KOTOBUKI.
I THOUGHT YOU WERE LOOKING FOR A JOB.
......
WOW, YOU GAVE IT QUITE A WORK-OVER.
YEAH, BUT...
Thanks, lady!
THERE'S STILL GOOD SOIL IF WE KEEP DIGGING.
It's a lot of work, though.
...THAT'S GOOD.
YOU HUNGRY?
HMM...
......
...

SHOKA?!
KOTOBUKI ...
...AND RAIMON!!
WHY...?
WHY DO WE KEEP BUMPING EACH OTHER?!
Waaaaaah
HE GOT ON HER BAD SIDE...
LOOKING FOR TSUBASA STILL? WHERE ARE YOU HEADED THIS TIME?
SHUT UP!!
I'M NOT TELLING YOU GUYS ANYTHING! YOU WONT GET THE BEST OF US ANYMORE!
Who's Who: Shoka
Occupation: Thief who handles explosives. She's set her sights on Tsubasa. She's a slow runner and has terrible aim. She blames Raimon for her bad luck. Poor woman, life hasn't been kind to her.
Relationship: Totally available. She's currently looking for a rich gentleman.
That devil is going to ruin everything for me again!
Waaah!
WE'RE READY TO GO TO SARABINA TO LOOK FOR CLUES TO TSUBASA WHEN YOU ARE.
Uh. Oops.
....
LET'S BE CLEAR ON THIS. IT WASN'T MY FAULT.

OKAY.
DUMA KURY. HE COMES FROM OLD MONEY.
HE SET UP THE SARABINA CULT SIX MONTHS AGO. THEY HAVE 30 FOLLOWERS SO FAR.
...AND THAT SYMBOL TOWER OF HIS. IT'S A WIND POWER STATION, ISN'T IT?
YES, THAT'S RIGHT.
WHAT IS THAT?
THAT REVOLVING THING IS AN ELECTRICITY GENERATING SYSTEM.
WHAT?!
Wind-driven power!
THAT'S INCREDIBLE.
A PRIVATE ELECTRIC GENERATOR IS NOT ILLEGAL. WHY HIDE IT ?
THE GENERATED ELECTRICITY RUNS DOWN TO THE BASEMENT.
WE GOT A THERMAL RESPONSE. THEY HAVE SOMETHING IN THE BASEMENT.
WAIT, ARE YOU INTERESTED IN IT BECAUSE IT'S CALLED "TSUBASA" CULT?
Please tell me you're not that naive.
YOU'RE A JERK, AND YOU ALWAYS HAVE BEEN.

And...
BOSS SAID IT'S NOT JUST AN ORDINARY TOWER. HER THIEF'S INSTINCT TOLD HER THAT...
I'VE TOLD YOU EVERYTHING. NOW, BEAT IT.
Shoot!!
GET OUT OF HERE, AND DON'T STAND IN MY WAY.
I'M NOT STANDING IN YOUR WAY.
YOU REALLY HAVE A BIG MOUTH.
ow...
I'M JUST STEPPING ON YOU BECAUSE YOU'RE IN MY WAY.
GOOD DAY.
GO TO HELL...
Welcome
Lunch & Dinner
...HEY...
お酒のおともにえだ豆
メニュー
WHAT DO YOU THINK SARABINA'S DOING, RUNNING ELECTRICITY IN THE BASEMENT?
NO IDEA. I DON'T WANT TO GET INVOLVED.

RIGHT?
WHA?!
It's him!
IT'S NICE TO SEE YOU AGAIN.
OKAY...
Why are you here?
YOU TWO MAKE A CUTE COUPLE.
YOU'RE A LOVELY YOUNG LADY...
!!
GET OFF, YOU TRANNIE!!
MASTER DUMA!!

I DON'T...
I DON'T LET...
...ANYONE BUT RAIMON TOUCH ME!!
ドカ
ドカ
WHAT AM I SAYING?
ドカ
...DOES YOUR LESSON INCLUDE WOOING WOMEN?
NO, OUR AIM IS TO SAVE THE WORLD WITH THE POWERS OF TSUBASA.
IF IT WEREN'T FOR HUMANS, THE EARTH WOULD BE ALIVE AND WELL. AND YOU WANT TO **SAVE** IT?
Not my business, though.
NATURAL DISASTERS WEREN'T NEW ON THIS PLANET EVEN WHEN CIVILIZATION FLOURISHED.
THAT MEANS THAT THE EARTH LIVES AT HER OWN PACE.
SHE'LL DIE WHEN SHE CHOOSES. HUMANS AREN'T EVEN IN THE PICTURE.
YOU'RE...
YOU'RE AN INCREDIBLY SELFISH MAN...

WHAT, DIDN'T YOU KNOW THAT?
DO I LOOK LIKE AN ANGEL?
Don't boast ...
AT LEAST...
I DON'T WANT SOMEONE WHO ENGAGES IN SOME DODGY BUSINESS IN THE BASEMENT TELLING ME WHAT TO DO.
...SO IT'S TRUE.
YOU'RE NOT TO BE UNDER-ESTIMATED...
RAIMON SHIRAGI.
I DIDN'T EVEN NOTICE THEM!!
YOU DON'T KNOW HOW SURPRISED I WAS...
?!
...TO SEE YOUR NAME IN THE ARMY'S DATABASE, WITH AN "E" ATTACHED TO IT.
I WONDER WHAT BRINGS AN ELITE OFFICER DOWN HERE?

!?
I can't believe I got an E!
!?
...YOU SEEM TO BE PRIVY TO A LOT OF INFO. YOU HAVE A COMPUTER IN THE BASEMENT OR SOMETHING?
MY GUESS IS THAT YOU HACKED INTO F, THE ARMY'S MOTHER COMPUTER.
NO CAN DO. I WANT TO KEEP A LOW PROFILE, YOU KNOW.
I'M AFRAID YOU HAVE NO CHOICE. I KNOW YOU WERE IN CHARGE OF TOP-SECRET MILITARY OPERATIONS.
THAT'S RIGHT. I'M HERE TO ASK YOU FOR HELP ABOUT IT.
AND YOU NO LONGER WORK FOR THEM. WE SEE THAT AS A CHANCE.
WE NEED YOUR HELP.
Wa--
--IT. HOLD IT, YOU...!
GAH!
CRAP!

NOW, COME WITH US.
I'M SO STUPID!!
RAIMON, DON'T LISTEN TO HIM!!
I DID IT AGAIN.
Raimon!!
DON'T BE SUCH A HERO!!
I'M DRAGGING HIM DOWN!!
...OKAY.
?!
DON'T LAY A FINGER ON KOTOBUKI.
WE WON'T, IF YOU DO YOUR JOB.
NO WORRIES, KOTOBUKI.
DO WHAT YOU WANT. I DON'T CARE!!
Buttface!!
RAIMON!!

NOW...
I HAVE...
...JUST THE PLACE FOR YOU...
Place
WIND POWER GENERATOR
Sarabina Tower.
OW!
IT'S A LITTLE CRAMPED.
TRY TO MAKE YOURSELF AT HOME.
BASTARD...
KOTOBUKI?

SHOKA!!
And the others!
YOU GUYS ARE BEING HELD HERE, TOO?
Ah ha ha ha!
SERVES HIM RIGHT!!
Gya ha, ha ha!
What a joke!
YOU'RE IN NO POSITION TO LAUGH!!
LOOK WHO'S TALKING! ANYWAY, WHERE'S RAIMON?!
What's with those two...?
DUMA GOT HIM.
Neighbors
STAY PUT.
YOU CAN'T DO ANYTHING.
JUST SIT PRETTY. THAT'S ALL YOU'RE GOOD FOR.
LET ME TELL YOU ONE THING...
RAIMON'S TOO GOOD FOR YOU.
I...

WHAT DO YOU KNOW, YOU DAMNED
TRANNIE!!
A TRANNIE...?
On what basis...?
パッタン
ガチャ
ガチャ
ガチャ
SHIT!
JUST CALM DOWN.
It won't open from inside.
SKYLIGHT!!
Hey...
WHY BOTHER? RAIMON WILL GET OUT OF THERE JUST FINE WITHOUT ANYONE'S HELP.
I really don't care, though.
I'LL SHOW HIM. THEY CALLED ME MONKEY FOR A REASON!
No!!
I'M NOT GOING TO LET THEM TAKE HIM AWAY!!
I CAN'T LET THEM HAVE RAIMON.
NOT EVEN FOR A MINUTE!!
Wow.
H-hey...

YOU JUST WATCH!!
"WHY ARE YOU UPSET?"
I DON'T WANT TO BE THE TAKER.
I WANT TO HELP HIM. I WANT TO...
...BE BETTER, AND...
...BECOME SOMEONE EVERYONE APPROVES OF.
I DON'T WANT TO JUST BE TOGETHER.
ガンガリリッ
GAAAH...
WATCH OUT...!
SO THAT I...
SO THAT...

...I CAN PROTECT RAIMON!!
Grr
Well...
I HATE TO SAY THIS, BUT THAT'S NOT PRETTY...
YEAH ...
HMPH.
DON'T RUSH YOURSELF UNLESS YOU HAVE A PLAN.
LET ME HELP YOU. WE CAN WORK SOMETHING OUT.
BOSS?
YES!!
WAIT!!
...WHY?
Huff
It's...
IT'S NOTHING.
Huff
I JUST WANT TO MAKE DUMA PAY FOR PUTTING ME IN THIS PLACE.

......
'K...
I HEARD THAT DUMA HAS A COMPUTER IN THE BASEMENT OF THE SARABINA TOWER.
I THINK THAT'S WHERE THEY TOOK RAIMON.
I see.
THEY'VE GOT A COMPUTER. THUS THE NEED FOR ELECTRICITY.
THIS IS THE MAP OF THE TOWER.
Skreee
DON'T DRAW WITH YOUR IRON NAIL!!
Shoka!
THERE IS ONLY ONE DOOR LEADING DOWN TO THE BASEMENT. IT'S NOT THAT COMPLICATED. IT'LL BE A QUICK TRIP.
1F →
Door to the basement
B1 →
Raimon.
Die, you idiot!
...THE COMPUTER CONTROLS THE DOOR, SO WE COULDN'T OPEN IT.
WE ALMOST MADE IT TO THE DOOR, BUT...
※ That's where they got caught.
BUT THERE'S EVEN BETTER WAY. IT'S THE POWER STATION.
AND WE'RE GOING TO SMASH THEM!!
Her eyes were...
...radiating as she spoke.
OKAY...

THE SARABINA TOWER'S HERE, AND THE WIND GENERATORS, AND THIS IS HERE.
Sara-bina tower
Wind generators
You're here.
WE'LL SET UP BOMBS IN THE GENERATORS.
KOTOBUKI, YOU'LL MAKE YOUR WAY TO THE DOOR AND WAIT. THREE MINUTES LATER, THE BOMBS WILL GO OFF, THE POWER WILL GO DOWN, AND YOU HEAD IN... ARE YOU LISTENING TO ME?!
ALL RIGHT. ALL RIGHT!
By the way...
STAY ALERT EVEN WHEN THE LIGHTS ARE OUT.
IT'S SAFE TO ASSUME THEY HAVE A BACKUP INSTALLED.
WHAT'S THAT?
THEY'LL HAVE A TEMPORARY ELECTRICITY SUPPLY. WHICH MEAN THE DOOR WILL CLOSE SHORTLY AFTER.
DON'T DILLY-DALLY. WHEN THE LIGHTS GO OUT, YOU GET IN THE DOOR. GOT IT?!
How can you be so ignorant? How long have you been a thief? How can you so ignorant?
I GOT IT. SO STOP SCRATCHING!!
Boss...
I TOOK CARE OF THE GUARDS.
AND I GOT OUR WEAPONS BACK.
NOW, LET'S GO TO THE POWER STATION!

HANG IN THERE, RAIMON.
Geez, why am I shaking...?
It's her iron nails...
IT'S PAYBACK TIME, TRANNIE!!
THANK YOU FOR YOUR PATIENCE...
RAIMON.
......
THAT'S SOME COMPUTER YOU'VE GOT HERE.
THANK YOU.
ANYTHING TO GET TO F.
IT GOT ME INFORMATION ON THE ARMY. I FOUND OUT A LOT ABOUT YOU, TOO, RAIMON.

HOWEVER, THERE'S ONE PROBLEM... THERE'S A POWERFUL BLOCK THAT'S PREVENTING ME FROM GOING FURTHER.
IT SEEMS IMPOSSIBLE TO BREAK. IT'S OBVIOUSLY IN A DIFFERENT LEAGUE.
IT'S TOP-SECRET. IT'S DESIGNED TO BE.
TRUE! I THINK THIS MUST BE WHERE THEY HID TSUBASA!
TSUBASA IS NOT JUST A MYTH.
THE ARMY MUST BE ONTO SOMETHING.
WHY HIDE IT? TSUBASA IS OUR ONLY CHANCE AT SAVING THE EARTH.
I DON'T KNOW, AND I DON'T EVEN WANT TO KNOW.
OKAY... BUT YOU STILL HAVE TO DESTROY THE BLOCK.
WE'RE HOLDING KOTOBUKI HOSTAGE, REMEMBER?
...THIS IS GETTING OLD.
IF YOU WANT TO SAVE THE WORLD, PLOW THE FIELDS AND PLANT SEEDS.

IF KOTOBUKI THOUGHT LIKE YOU...
...THAT WOULD BE WHAT SHE'D DO.
SHE DOESN'T HAVE AN AGENDA LIKE ME.
SHE NEVER STOPS TRYING.
LIKE IT'S THE MOST NATURAL THING TO DO.
フォン…
...IF YOU DON'T WANT TO SEE HER DAMAGED, GET ON WITH IT.
I SAID DON'T TOUCH HER.
ピ
ピ ピ
...OH, NO.
WE NEED A FOLK SONG OF HYOTAN ISLAND TO BREAK THE PASSWORD.
ピ ピ
HUH?!
Hyotan? What's that?
YOU DON'T KNOW? IT'S AN ISLAND OF AN ANCIENT COUNTRY CALLED JAPAN.
Wh--
I'VE NEVER HEARD OF SUCH A--

GOTCHA.
STOP THAT.
OKAY, BUT YOU'D BETTER BE HAPPY WHEN WE GET IN.
SAY THAT AGAIN WHEN YOU HAVE BROKEN INTO THE SYSTEM. IT MUST BE A HARD TASK EVEN FOR YOU...
NOT AT ALL. I WAS THE ONE WHO...
...CREATED THIS BLOCK.
AS PART OF RESEARCH I DID WHEN I WAS 17.
RE--
RE-SEARCH ...?
WHEN YOU WERE 17...?
THIS TIME IT'S TRUE.

IS EVERYTHING IN ORDER?
YES, SIR...
?!
WHAT'S THAT?!
!!
DID YOU KILL THEM?
OF COURSE NOT. THEY'RE JUST GOING TO BE OUT FOR A WHILE.
GET THEM OUT.
I installed a fresh magazine.
Just light it before you shoot.
KOTOBUKI, YOU KNOW WHAT TO DO. YOU HAVE THREE MINUTES.
GET TO THE DOOR AND...GO INSIDE WHEN THE LIGHT GOES OUT.
SURE!
IF I FIND ANYTHING ABOUT TSUBASA, I WILL TAKE IT WITH ME.
YOU DO THAT, PLEASE. NOW GO!

WOW, I DIDN'T KNOW HELPING OTHERS WAS IN YOUR NATURE, BOSS.
Are you sure you're not sick?
SHE MAY BE DUMB, BUT SHE'S A GOOD GIRL...
IT'S HARD NOT TO LIKE SOMEONE LIKE THAT!!
I'M INSIDE THE TOWER...
しゅたっ
...HEAD STRAIGHT.
Crud. There are guards...
I'VE GOT ONE MINUTE LEFT.
Safe...
ザワ
ザワ
MAKE A TURN THERE...
...AND...
"I'M JUST STEPPING ON YOU BECAUSE YOU'RE IN MY WAY."

LET'S STEP ON THEM!!
WHAT?!
DID YOU... FAIL?!
WHA--
IT'S PROGRAMMED THAT WAY. NO ACCESS FROM OUTSIDE IS ALLOWED.
EVEN IF YOU GOT THE PASSWORD RIGHT...
...THE BLOCK WILL BE TURNED INTO A VIRUS.
IN 30 SECONDS, THE VIRUS WILL REACH YOUR COMPUTER...
...AND EAT IT UP.
IT WILL IDENTIFY THE LOCATION AND NOTIFY F IMMEDIATELY.

NO REGRETS.
THIS IS WHY YOU DIDN'T PUT UP A FIGHT.
YOU HAD THIS PLANNED FROM THE BEGINNING...
DIDN'T I TELL YOU?
DID YOU THINK YOU'D GET AWAY WITH IT?
AFTER YOU KISSED MY KOTOBUKI?
!
QUIT SCURRYING AROUND...
YOU MUST BE DUMA'S ENEMY!
I CAN SEE THE DOOR...
RAIMON'S DOWN THERE...

I HAVE TO GET TO THE DOOR SOON...!!
SEVEN SECONDS LEFT.
6
5
4
3
KA-CHAK
ガチッ
DO YOU WANT TO DIE?!
ビクッ
2
?!
BEEP
BACKUP SYSTEM IS ONLINE.

STOP RIGHT THERE.
YOU DON'T WASTE ANY TIME DO YOU?
WHAT A TIMELY BLACKOUT... THE VIRUS IS DEAD.
IT LOOKS LIKE I AM IN LUCK.
FINE BY ME.
I'VE GOT KOTOBUKI.

WHAT?
OH!
WHO'S THAT MAN LAYING THERE?
I SHOT HIM IN THE STOMACH ONCE, AND HE WENT FLYING INTO THE DOOR AND BROKE IT.
KOTOBUKI, YOU'RE HURT...
DON'T TOUCH ME!!
YOU'RE A REAL PIECE OF WORK.
I KNEW YOU'D BE ABLE TO GET YOURSELF OUT...
...BUT...
...YOU HAD ME SO WORRIED WHILE YOU WERE GONE...
YOU TOLD ME NOT TO WALK AWAY, AND LOOK WHAT YOU'VE DONE!!

I'M SORRY I HURT YOU.
RAIMON...
WHEN WE GET HOME, I'M GOING TO KISS EVERY PART OF YOUR BODY THAT HURTS.
I'LL KILL YOU IF YOU TRY THAT...
RAIMON...
YOU HURT HER, TOO, DIDN'T YOU?
OH...
がす
NO!!
THE VIRUS IS ALIVE...
?
OF COURSE.
YOU REALLY THOUGHT THAT MY VIRUS WOULD BE DESTROYED BY A MERE BLACKOUT?
THE VIRUS IS COMING...
I'M DEAD.

HELLO!
I'M THE VIRUS'S CUTE LITTLE ANGEL, HERE TO PROTECT DATA FROM BAD PEOPLE!
HEY, YOU! YOU SHOULDN'T VIOLATE OTHER PEOPLE'S PRIVACY!
That is a big no-no.
I'M ALMOST AFRAID TO ASK... IS THAT ME?
Big no-no, my ass!
I MADE THIS WHEN I JUST MET YOU. YOU WERE SO ADORABLE. I JUST HAD TO USE YOU AS A MODEL.
It's cute, huh?
OH, AND THE ARMY IS GOING TO BE ONTO YOU.
THIS IS GOING TO BE A BIG TEARFUL REUNION.
IS THIS THE BEST YOU COULD DO?!
Very personal!
Kya ha ha!
I AM GOING TO PUNISH YOU, BAD BOY.
READY?!

SO LET'S DESTROY IT.
WHA
Uh...
YOU CAN STOP NOW! ONE MORE BLAST, AND THE TOWER WILL EXPLODE!
OH REALLY?
SOUNDS LIKE FUN TO ME.
IT'S NOT FUN AT ALL!!
THE TOWER IS GONE...
That's amazing...
IT'S RAIMON.
?!
DESTROYER!

NO NEED TO BE ANGRY. EVERYONE'S FINE.
And I only had to save Kotobuki.
DO YOU HAVE TO MAKE EVERYTHING SPECTACULAR?!!
Raimon!!
デュマ
WH--
WHAT'S HAPPENING, RAIMON?!
DON'T ASK ME.
SHOKA.
YOU--!!
WHY DID YOU DESTROY THE TOWER?
WHAT IF THEY HAD A LEAD ON TSUBASA?!
BECAUSE DUMA HURT KOTOBUKI.
what he gets.
OH!
OW...
C--
CRAZY NOISE FROM BELOW...
W-WHAT IS THIS?!
AH!

HUH...?
WHAT'S ...?
IT'S WARM...
IT'S A HOT SPRING...
HOT SPRING?
KYA!
Gasp
HOT WATER FROM DEEP IN THE EARTH IS EXPLODING OUT OF THE GROUND!
Came around
YOU MEAN...
THE EARTH IS STILL WARM...
I GUESS SO.
IT'S WARM. THAT'S PROOF OF LIFE, RIGHT?
UH-HUH.
HEY, TRANNIE. YOU HEAR THAT?

IT'S NOT DEAD!
THE EARTH IS VERY MUCH ALIVE.
WE CAN PLANT SEEDS.
WE CAN RESTORE FORESTS AND MOUNTAINS.
どげし
DO YOU WANT ANYTHING ELSE FROM US?
N--
NO...
YOU'D BETTER NOT SHOW THAT STUPID FACE OF YOURS AGAIN.
Oh?
RAIMON...
YOU'RE NOT GOING TO TURN ME IN?
GO AHEAD AND TURN YOURSELF IN.
DOESN'T MATTER TO ME.

Raimon's shoes are very hard.

...
BESIDES, ALL THE EVIDENCE IS GONE ALONG WITH THE EXPLOSION.
I didn't mean it to happen.
......
Heh...
GEEZ...
HE'S SO SELFISH...
AND SO IS THE PLANET...
I am...
I'M SORRY...
I COULDN'T FIND A LEAD ON TSUBASA.

IT'S FINE. I HAD GIVEN UP HOPE FOR FINDING ANYTHING THE MOMENT THAT DEVIL SHOWED UP.
...YOU TWO KIND OF...
...I THINK.
...LOOK GOOD TOGETHER.
WELL, GOOD LUCK.
Eek!
BOSS, RAIMON'S COMING!!
Let's go!
THERE'S BEEN ENOUGH DAMAGE FOR ONE DAY!!
WHERE'S SHOKA?
SHE RA-- SHE'S GONE.
どあ~
Wait up, guys! Don't leave me behind!
Shake those legs, boss.
Well, anyway...
THIS GUY'LL GIVE US A LIFT TO THE NEXT VILLAGE.
HUH?!
Ye--
YES, SIR, MY PLEASURE!!
HE BLACK-MAILED HIM...
HM?
NOTHING...

Now...
I'M GOING TO FIND WORK IN THE NEXT TOWN!
FIRST THING'S FIRST.
TELL ME EVERY SINGLE PART WHERE IT HURTS.
Oh?
WHAT FOR...?
Oh, that's...
!!
SHOULD I START WITH YOUR FACE?
YOUR HANDS? OR LEGS?
NOOO!!
WE MADE A PROMISE.
Keep it down...
STOP TRYING TO TRICK ME!!
Duma, a few days later.
Cheap! Sarabina Springs
Massage service available
WELCOME.
Towel
Eggs
WE'RE JUST GOING TO GO AND PLOW.

翼を持つ者

Adelite's Path

This is the girl who has received my undivided love, and she's going to make her first appearance in the third episode. To tell you the truth, I wanted to make her appear in the first episode, but when I finished plotting the story, my initial plan of her, her brother, and butler showing up had been eliminated. (laughter) And when I thought maybe this could be the chance to make them appear, I didn't have time to make it happen. It's sad, really.

There's another character I had to give up for a while after the second episode: Shoka. She was supposed to be a regular, but circumstances forced me to decide otherwise...

Here's Shoka in a maid costume.

Get me out of this outfit!

WILSON HOUSE...
THEY PUT OUT AN AD LOOKING FOR A MAID.
THAT MEANS THEY'LL AT LEAST TALK TO ME.
Yeah!
BRING IT ON!!
EASY, KOTOBUKI. YOU'RE NOT GOING TO WAR OR ANYTHING.
BUT I CAN'T HELP IT. OPPORTUNITY HAS FINALLY KNOCKED.
I'VE GOT TO ACT FAST BEFORE SOMEONE BEATS ME TO IT.
Oh.
DON'T WORRY ABOUT THAT.
I TORE THE AD OFF THE WALL.
You won't have any competition.
Wanted: Maid
RAIMON...!
That's wrong...
WE ARE IN THE 22ND CENTURY.
THERE WERF SO MANY WARS...
...THAT CAUSED THE EARTH TO DRY UP.

ONLY THE RICH, THE ARMY, AND THE POLITICIANS HAVE ACCESS TO THE NICER AMENITIES.
MEANWHILE, ORDINARY PEOPLE LIVE IN POVERTY, AND THE STREETS ARE FILLED WITH CRIMINALS.
I LIVED AS A THIEF IN ORDER TO SURVIVE...
...BUT THAT'S ALL BEHIND ME, NOW.
I'VE BEEN TRAVELING FROM TOWN TO TOWN, LOOKING FOR A JOB.
SOMEONE'S HERE FOR AN INTERVIEW.
knock
knock
THIS IS MY CHANCE!
ゴク
ガチャ
WELCOME.
MY NAME IS ADELITE WILSON.
Oh?
What if it's someone like this?
But...
Heh heh heh...

I AM THE ONLY DAUGHTER OF THE FAMILY.
I AM GOING TO INTERVIEW YOU ON BEHALF OF MY LATE FATHER.
WOW.
WHOA, YOU'RE...
Heh...
HONESTY WON'T WIN YOU ANYTHING, HONEY.
HUH?
SHE'S RIGHT, KOTOBUKI. YOU KNOW WHAT THEY SAY... A CHILD PRODIGY'S A NOBODY AFTER AGE 20.
ONCE AGAIN... HUH?
She doesn't get it.
TWITCH
RAIMON USED TO BE AN ELITE OFFICER IN THE ARMY.
...WHO IS THAT?
YOUR FRIEND?!
YEAH.
HE'D CHASE AFTER ME IN HIS OWN FUSSY WAY WHEN I WAS A THIEF.

HE QUIT FOUR AND A HALF MONTHS AGO, THOUGH.
HE SAID...
"ALL I WANTED WAS TO END THE WHOLE OFFICER-THIEF THING AND BE WITH YOU."
Four and a half months ago.
SINCE THEN, WE'VE BEEN ON THE ROAD.
YOUR BOYFRIEND?
ずばリ
WHAT?!
WELL, UM...
Erm...
I STILL CAN'T GET USED TO THAT IDEA.
NO, IT'S NOT THAT.
WE ARE SOUL MATES.
ブギュ
ANYWAY!!
Okay.
I'VE GOT THE SPEED...
ZIP
...AND THE STRENGTH!
Hmph
AND I CAN UNLOCK ANYTHING. HIRE ME!!
In a matter of three seconds.
YOU'LL MAKE AN EXCELLENT THIEF.
I need a maid.
I GET THAT A LOT! BUT LISTEN, I'M NOT THE TYPE!!
NOT ANOTHER WORD.
You're a bad liar.
HAVING FUN?

IS THIS YOUR NEW MAID?
MOTHER...
THIS IS MY MOM.
AND THAT'S DR. KAMIHARA. HE'S A SCIENTIST.
...HELLO.
HERE'S A LITTLE SOMETHING FOR YOU.
Press the button, and it will speak.
OH, MY. THANKS.
That's life.
THAT'S ANOTHER CREATION FROM DR. KAMIHARA. ISN'T IT GREAT?
HE'S WORKING ON A TSUBASA DETECTOR RIGHT NOW, AND I'M SPONSORING HIM.
WHEN IT'S DONE, WE'LL FIND TSUBASA AND WE WILL MAKE A LOT OF MONEY.
HE'S MAKING A DETECTOR...
How's that
IT'S EASY TO JUST NAME IT THAT...
MOTHER!! DON'T START ON THAT AGAIN!!
That's life.
HUH? WHY? THERE'S NOTHING WRONG WITH BELIEVING IN TSUBASA.
THAT'S NOT THE POINT.
TSUBASA IS A MYTH.

IT'S SAID THAT TSUBASA GRANTED EVERYONE'S WISHES.
NOBODY KNOWS WHAT IT LOOKS LIKE OR WHERE IT COMES FROM, BUT PEOPLE BELIEVE IT STILL LIES SOMEWHERE IN THE GROUND.
WHOEVER FINDS IT WILL HAVE HIS WISH GRANTED.
じろ
じろ
にやり
Eh?!
WHAT'S UP WITH HIM...?
OKAY THEN, MY LADY. I WILL EXCUSE MYSELF. I WILL KEEP YOU POSTED.
Please do!!
I'M JUST GOING TO SHOW HIM OUT.
WATCH YOUR STEP...
That's life.
ガシャーン
OH, MY.
Oh no!
I TRIPPED OVER SOMETHING.
パタン
....
ブチッ
That's-
GOD, THAT WOMAN REALLY TESTS ME.

HOW CAN SHE BELIEVE IN A MYTH? TSUBASA IS JUST FICTION
AND SHE'S WILLING TO SPONSOR THAT FRAUD.
IT SEEMS...
EH?
...THAT THEY DON'T GET ALONG.
THAT WOMAN IS USELESS.
SO I'M GOING TO DECIDE: YOU'RE HIRED.
WE DON'T HAVE ANY OTHER CHOICE. YOU WERE THE ONLY APPLICANT.
......!!
Y...
YIPPEE!!
WHO SAID ANYTHING ABOUT HIRING YOU?!

AND SO...
OKAY, KOTOBUKI. YOU START WORK TOMORROW.
Yeah!
ASK ME ANYTHING!!
AS FOR RAIMON... ADY SAID YOU CAN DO WHATEVER...
HM.
It's a man.
Very nice.
ADY NEEDED TO GET HIRED HELP, WITH MOST OF THE ORIGINAL HOUSEKEEPERS GONE.
HER FATHER WAS AN EXECUTIVE AT A FABRIC MANUFACTURING COMPANY. EVER SINCE HE WAS KILLED IN A CAR ACCIDENT SIX MONTHS AGO...
You know.
...THINGS HAVE BEEN TOUGH FOR THE WILSONS.
We're feeling the pinch, too.
OH...
"ON BEHALF OF MY LATE FATHER...!"
AS YOU'RE AWARE, THE LADY OF THE HOUSE IS NOT DEPENDABLE. SHE DOESN'T KNOW A THING ABOUT KEEPING FAMILY TOGETHER.
HOW CAN SHE BELIEVE IN TSUBASA AND THAT DODGY SCIENTIST? THAT'S JUST INSANE, DON'T YOU THINK?
You saw her, right?!
BUT ADELITE SEEMS SMART.
SHE'S A KNOW-IT-ALL. SHE DOESN'T TALK LIKE AN 11-YEAR-OLD CHILD.
SHE'LL NEVER GET MY SYMPATHY.

YOU'LL FIND OUT WHAT I'M TALKING ABOUT TOMORROW.
Kya!
He's come back from a room allocated for him.
GRAB
!!
......
WHAT WAS THAT?!
Out of the blue.
WELL, YOU LOOKED LIKE YOU NEEDED CHEERING UP.
Hmph.
WHAT ARE YOU TALKING ABOUT...?
I JUST GOT A JOB. IT'S A DREAM COME TRUE FOR ME.
A job with a room and three meals! How can you ask for more?!!
ANYWAY, WHAT MADE YOU COME HERE?
But I insist!!
I'M GOING TO WORK MY BUTT OFF AND CLEAR UP MY DEBT!!
Raimon's been paying for the food and she wants to pay it back.
I'VE BEEN TELLING YOU, YOU DON'T HAVE TO DO THAT...
TO BE WITH YOU.
What else?

むく
Sorry I asked...
GOOD FOR YOU.
YOU'VE GOT A JOB.
HAPPY?
......
WE HAVE A BIG DAY TOMORROW!!
すっく
I'm going to bed!!
YEAH, LET'S.
ポンポン
ハハー
I WAS HOPING I COULD GET HER IN THE MOOD...
SOMETIMES I THINK...
RAIMON SPOILS ME TOO MUCH!!
I THINK!!
I JUST WANT TO BECOME GOOD ENOUGH FOR HIM. SOMEONE HE CAN COUNT ON!
BUT IT'S ALWAYS RAIMON WHO'S DOING THE PROTECTING.
LIKE WHEN HE WOULDN'T LET ME...

...SPEND MY OWN MONEY FOR HIM.
I'll get you a new outfit.
I'll buy it myself!!
In other words, he tricked her into buying it.
BUT...
I WANT TO DO SOMETHING NICE FOR HIM.
WHEN I'VE EARNED ENOUGH MONEY...
...I WANT TO SPEND IT ON HIM...
...AND MAKE HIM HAPPY.
HOLD ON!!
HE MIGHT FIND IT EASIER TO ACCEPT IF IT ISN'T MONEY!!
YES! I COULD GIVE HIM A PRESENT!!
Right on, Kotobuki!!
All right!
LET'S START WITH ASKING HIM WHAT HE WANTS. AND DO IT SUBTLY.
LET'S WORK HARD!!
shoes on the bed!

"I'VE BEEN GETTING SOME LOW QUALITY SILK, LATELY."
"YOU MEAN, THERE'S A VENDOR TRYING TO CHEAT YOU?"
"OUR COMPANY'S THROWING A PARTY NEXT MONTH. YOU SHOULD COME. WE'LL GET YOU A NEW DRESS."
"REALLY?! THAT'S WONDERFUL!!"
"...I'M WORRIED."
"YOUR MOM CAN MAKE YOU ONE."
"OH, NO. I'M TERRIBLE WITH A NEEDLE AND THREAD. NO MATTER HOW HARD I TRY, I CAN'T GET IT DONE."
"RIGHT. YOU HAVE CLUMSY HANDS."
"MY LADY!!"
"ADY!! THERE WAS AN ACCIDENT AND MASTER WAS...!!"

"THE CLIFF CRUMBLED DOWN..."
"I WONDER IF THE LADY OF THE HOUSE WILL BE ABLE TO KEEP THE FAMILY TOGETHER..."
"MOTHER!! WHAT IS THIS MONEY FOR?!"
"IT'S FOR DR. KAMIHARA. ONCE WE HAVE THE TSUBASA DETECTOR UP AND RUNNING, WE WON'T HAVE TO WORRY ABOUT MONEY."
"I'M SORRY, MY LADY, BUT WE QUIT."
"MOTHER, YOU SHOULD STOP SPONSORING HIM. WE'LL BE BROKE IF YOU DON'T."
Wanted: Maid
"IT'S ALL RIGHT."
どん!
BANG!

NO.
DON'T LOOK AT ME.
I KNOW I LOOK WEIRD!!
HOW CUTE!
YOU'RE SO LOVELY. I'M AROUSED.
Huh?!
You're kidding, right?
IT'S JUST A COSTUME!!
OKAY, LET'S GET TO WORK.
RAIMON, YOU'RE IN THE BACK...
OH!!

RAIMON, YOU'RE...
HM?
UM. I DON'T KNOW HOW TO START...
UM... IS THERE ANYTHING...
...YOU WANT...?
YOU.
ASIDE FROM ME.
IT HAS TO BE A THING. A PHYSICAL THING.
YOU KNOW, SOMETHING YOU WANT TO OWN.
I WANT YOU.
In many ways.
FORGET IT!!
THAT'S NOT WHAT I ASKED!!
......
HE'S A TOUGH NUT TO CRACK.
I should have seen that coming.
SWITCH TO PLAN B. I'LL FIGURE IT OUT ON MY OWN.
WHAT WOULD IT BE...?
......
Heh.

Anyway...
THIS IS SO MUCH FUN.
It's like a real job.
MOTHER?
KNOCK
KNOCK
KNOCK
MOTHER?
KNOCK
MOTHE--
キィ…
Kyaah!
NO!!
DON'T COME IN. GO AWAY!!
CLOSE THE DOOR!!
A LETTER FROM FATHER'S COMPANY.
OH.
OOPS.
Ah!
GIVE ME THAT!
THEN YOU SHOULD JUST ANSWER ME OR KEEP THE DOOR LOCKED.
YOU'RE RIGHT.
WHAT IS IT, DEAR?
ERM.
WELL...

IT'S AN INVITATION TO MR. PRESIDENT'S 60TH BIRTHDAY PARTY.
Really?
HOW NICE.
DON'T YOU GET IT? WE CAN'T AFFORD SOMETHING LIKE THIS ANYMORE.
YOU CAN SEND A MESSAGE CARD.
WHAT SHOULD I WRITE?
CONGRATU-LATIONS ON YOUR 60TH BIRTHDAY.
I PRAY THAT YOU WILL HAVE MANY MORE BIRTHDAYS TO COME.
WE ARE SORRY TO INFORM YOU THAT WE CANNOT PAY OUR COMPLIMENTS...
HUH?
...I'LL DO IT.
OH, AND, ABOUT DR. KAMIHARA...
AGAIN? I'M NOT PULLING THE PLUG.
I KNOW WE HAVE SOMETHING GOOD HERE.
AND...

IS THERE ANY OTHER WAY?
WELL...
........!!
Then...
I'LL WAIT FOR YOUR REPLY.
......
......
KYaaah!!
WHAT?!
Oh.
SORRY.
KYaaah!
WATCH OUT!!
WHAT ARE YOU DOING UP THERE?!!
Geez...
YOU MAY LEAVE THAT AREA...
.....

ADY... DO YOU HATE YOUR MOM?
YOU WERE WATCHING US.
SHE HATES ME.
YOU SAW IT. SHE WOULDN'T LET ME IN.
NOT THAT I CARE. I JUST HOPE...
...SHE STAYS OUT OF TROUBLE.
THAT'S ALL I ASK.
I HAVE NEVER BEEN AND WILL NEVER BE...
...A CHILD.
SO WHAT ABOUT THE PARTY?
IT'S JUST NOISE. I HATE PARTIES.
BUT SHE LOOKED...
...A LITTLE...
SHE'S DEFINITELY SMART FOR AN 11-YEAR-OLD KID.
Now...
IT'S FOODTIME!
......
KOTOBUKI, AREN'T YOU HUNGRY?

Omelet
WOW!!
IT'S TO DIE FOR!!
MR. SHIRAGI.
Oh ♥
THERE'RE SO MANY THINGS I HAVE TO DO.
The omelet is a big bonus.
SIT, SIT!
Hi.
HOW WAS YOUR FIRST DAY?
GREAT.
GOOD.
YOUR...
...BANDANA DOESN'T MATCH YOUR OUTFIT.
Really?
THIS FEELS RIGHT FOR ME.
Can it really be called a bandana, though?
No idea.
I GOT IT!!
Kyaaah! ♥
DON'T TELL ME YOU'LL TURN VIOLENT WHEN YOU TAKE IT OFF.
THAT'S RIGHT.
HEH HEH...
Kyaaah!

I DON'T KNOW WHAT CAME OVER YOU. YOU ALMOST KNOCKED THE TABLE OVER!
Oh!
SORRY ABOUT THAT.
IT'S FINE AS LONG AS THERE'S FOOD FOR ME AND KOTOBUKI.
YOU ALL RIGHT?
YEAH. I'M FINE.
THAT'S IT. A BANDANA!!
KOTOBUKI.
IT'S NOT MUCH BUT IT'S A START!!
...SILLY GIRL.
IT'S MORE FUN TO WORK...
...WHEN YOU HAVE A CLEAR GOAL.
OH?

IT'S ADY... WHAT'S SHE LOOKING AT?
THAT'S...
...HER MOM'S ROOM.
!
...I WONDER IF...
...ADY KNOWS SHE LOOKS...
...SO LONELY.
NOT THAT I WOULD TELL HER THAT...
B-
BUT... SHOULD I...
OH!
Hold on.
ADY!!
Huff Huff
TEA.
I BROUGHT YOU TEA...
Huff
Huff
...I DIDN'T ASK.
NO, BUT I WANTED TO...UH...
SORRY, I JUST RAN HERE...
Huff
Huff
It's hard...
Huff

HEH
YOU ARE AN ODD GIRL. OKAY, I'LL HAVE THE TEA.
HM?
OH!
Do you even know how to brew tea? You ruined the flavor.
And my favorite is Assam!!
Okay...
WAIT!
RAIMON AND ADY'S MOM?
...AND I SAW YOU WEARING AN OLD BANDANA.
SO I GOT YOU A NEW ONE.
...I DON'T WANT IT.
WHAT?
NOT MY CUP OF TEA.

WAIT A MINUTE!!
...WHAT'S THE MATTER?
...THAT WAS MY IDEA.
I WAS GOING TO GIVE HIM A BANDANA.
"NOT MY CUP OF TEA."
YOU'RE A COUPLE, RIGHT?
THEN HE'S HAPPY JUST TO HAVE YOU.
WHY DON'T YOU LEAVE IT THAT WAY?

I DON'T CARE ABOUT PRESENTS.
I'VE NEVER HAD ONE.
"YOUR MOM COULDN'T MAKE YOU A DRESS."
"THAT'S OKAY. THE DRESS YOU BOUGHT FOR ME IS MUCH BETTER."
NOT EVEN A DRESS.
"I'M SORRY..."
Ah ha ha...
"WHAT A LOVELY DRESS!"
"MOM MADE IT..."
"...JUST FOR ME."
"ISN'T IT WONDERFUL?"
......!!

KYAAAAH!!
ADY?!
WHAT?
THE CRYSTAL OUR FAMILY HAS CHERISHED FOR GENERATIONS IS GONE...!!
CRYSTAL?
WE HAD IT FITTED IN THE CEILING.
WHY...? WHERE DID IT GO?
KAMIHARA...!!
?
OF COURSE. IT'S HIM.
HE WAS ALWAYS EYEING IT.
HE'S SO GOING TO PAY!!
WAIT... DO YOU HAVE PROOF?
PROOF CAN FOLLOW LATER.
I'M NOT GOING TO LET HIM GET AWAY WITH IT!!

ADY, WAIT! CALM DOWN, WILL YOU?!
I AM BEING CALM!!
FINE.
SUIT YOURSELF.
I CAN'T LEAVE HER LIKE THIS.
LET ME HELP!!
I'M COMING WITH YOU!!
...BUT THIS DOESN'T CONCERN YOU.
I KNOW THIS IS UNCALLED FOR.
JUST LET ME!!
SO THIS...
...IS HIS HOUSE. IT LOOKS SUSPICIOUS.
THAT'S WHAT I'VE BEEN SAYING FROM DAY ONE.

AT LEAST YOU DIDN'T BRING THAT WEIRD MAN WITH YOU. GOOD THINKING.
...I DIDN'T TELL HIM.
Avoiding.
I COULDN'T FACE HIM...
He doesn't do work.
IF I DON'T HAVE TO DO ANYTHING TO MAKE HIM HAPPY...
...THEN WOULD IT BE BEST TO LEAVE IT THAT WAY?
IT'S BETTER THAN MESSING UP AND CAUSING HIM TROUBLE.
MAYBE I'LL JUST LET HIM SPOIL ME.
BUT...
...COULD I REALLY JUST LET HIM DO THAT?
Okay.
LET'S GO.
Wow!
AN EXPAND-ABLE LADDER!!
I WANTED ONE WHEN I WAS A THIEF, BUT I DIDN'T HAVE THAT KIND OF MONEY...
*The electric version

WHAT'S THIS...?
WHAT A WEIRD PLACE...
THE CRYSTAL.
BEEP
WHERE IS IT?
BEEEP
KYAAAH!!
INTRUDERS!!
?!
...!
WH- WHAT?!
WAIT, THAT'S A ROBOT!!
WHAT'S GOING ON?!
WELL, WELL, WELL...

KAMIHARA...
WE KNOW THAT YOU TOOK THE CRYSTAL!!
YOU GOT ME.
I KNEW IT!
...YOU SHOULD TRY AND DENY IT FIRST...
THE CRYSTAL IS ABSOLUTELY NECESSARY TO MAKE MY DETECTOR WORK.
THE INDEX OF REFRACTION IS SIO_2. THE CRYSTAL HAS A SUPERIOR QUALITY.
THIS IS NATURAL. A RARITY NOWADAYS. WHAT DO YOU SAY? CAN I HOLD ONTO THIS FOR A WHILE?
HOW CAN YOU BE SO COOL ABOUT IT!
I WANT IT BACK NOW!!
HOW SAD...
I'M ONLY TALKING ABOUT THE GREATEST INVENTION OF THE CENTURY.
HOW INTER-ESTING.
TELL ME HOW IT WORKS.

RAI--
YOU WERE FOLLOWING US?!!
Oh no!! Someone else broke in!
I SAW YOU GOING OUT.
HERE'S YOUR LUNCH.
Kyaah!
Kyaah!
Kyaah!
YOUR GREATEST INVENTION, THAT IS.
Kyaah!
Kyaah!
Kyaah!
Kyaah!
Kyaah!
Kyaah!
SHUT UP.
Agh! ♥
MY LITTLE REMI!!
My little Remi?!

Remil...
YOUR NAME SOUNDED FAMILIAR.
YOU USED TO INVENT ONE USELESS WEAPON AFTER ANOTHER. IT TICKED THE ARMY OFF EVERY TIME.
YOU WERE AN IMBECILE THEN, YOU'RE AN IMBECILE NOW.
HOW...DO YOU KNOW ALL THIS...? ABOUT THE ARMY AND STUFF...
BECAUSE I'M A GENIUS.
WHAT DO YOU MEAN?
LOOK, I DON'T CARE WHATEVER CRAP YOU PULL, JUST LEAVE KOTOBUKI OUT OF IT.
For that reason I have to make you pay.
Mwa ha ha...
THAT'S NONSENSE. YOU GOT ANY EVIDENCE? I'M JUST A SCIENTIST WHO'S TRYING TO MAKE A DIFFERENCE IN THE WORLD.
Heh...
I'M AFRAID NOBODY BUT ME CAN GET IT MOVIN--
WE'LL SEE ABOUT THAT WHEN WE LAUNCH YOUR MACHINE.
カタ
Wha--!
HOW DID YOU BREAK MY SECRET PASSWORD...?
カタ
I'M A GENIUS.

どかーん
KYAAAH!!
IT'S OKAY. NO ONE LIVES THERE.
......
ボ
......
IT'S--
IT'S JUST A WEAPON!!
YOU LIED TO US!!
Damn.
IT'S YOUR FAULT. YOU LET ME DECEIVE YOU!!
WHY WOULD I LISTEN TO THAT BITCH?!
SHE WAS AN EASY TARGET. YOU'D BE BETTER OFF WITHOUT HER.
SHE'S NOT FIT TO BE A MOTHER.
HE'S RIGHT. SHE'S NEVER BEEN A GOOD MOTHER.
I DON'T CARE ABOUT TSUBASA. I WAS IN IT FOR THE MONEY AND THE CHANCE TO USE MY TALENTS.
WHAT'S THE PROBLEM? I THOUGHT YOU HATED YOUR MOTHER.
HEY!!

SHE DOESN'T KNOW HOW TO TREAT A CHILD. SHE CAN'T EVEN CHANGE A DIAPER.
SHE'S CLUELESS, CLUMSY, AND SHALLOW.
SHE CAN'T EVEN MAKE A DRESS...
I NEVER WENT TO ANOTHER PARTY.
I'VE BEEN WAITING.
I'VE BEEN WAITING...
...FOR THE DAY WHERE I CAN SMILE LIKE THAT.
BUT...I'M DONE WAITING.
I DON'T EXPECT ANYTHING FROM HER...
ADY.
IN TRUTH...
YOU KEPT YOUR TINY SELF ALL BOTTLED UP, DIDN'T YOU?
I'VE SEEN THE LOOK...
...THAT SAYS "LOOK AT ME."
OH, NO, YOU DON'T.

!!
AGH!
HUH...?!
TWO...
...KOTO-BUKIS ...?!
Nn?
THAT WAS SCARY.
KOTO-BUKI...?
UGH...

EH?
What?!
WHAT AM I DOING...?!
YOU OUGHT TO PROTECT ME.
Hey... I'm over here.
IF YOU LOVE ME, THEN SHOW IT.
YOU'RE HAPPY AS LONG AS I'M HERE, RIGHT?
!
SHE'S WRONG!!
WHAT THE HELL IS SHE SAYING? SHE'S SO FULL OF IT!
AM I RIGHT?
NO!! THIS IS NOT RIGHT AT ALL!!
THAT'S NOT ME!! IT'S NOT!
"I WONDER WHAT IT'S LIKE TO BE SPOILED?"
SHUT UP!!

IT'S NOT ME!!
Oh, no!
THAT'S MY NEW ROBOT IN PROGRESS!!
That hurt a bit...
BE CAREFUL WITH THAT FIST OF YOURS! WHAT IF YOU WERE WRONG?
ビボン
WHA--?!
THEY DON'T LOOK ANYTHING ALIKE.
THIS IS AN INSULT.
RIGHT.
BUT WHY KOTOBUKI...?
I knew you were a pervert.
I LIKE THE WAY SHE LOOKS.
What are you--?!
STOP THAT!!

YOU CAN'T JUST QUIETLY WALK AWAY AFTER HURTING KOTOBUKI.
DIDN'T YOU KNOW THAT?
NO, I DID NO--
TOO BAD.
WELL, HE DESERVES IT...
Gyaaaaah!!
......
IT'S ALL RIGHT TO MAKE A MISTAKE...
OH?
THE FIRST TIME IS TRICKY.
BUT IT WON'T STOP ME...
I'LL KEEP TRYING UNTIL I CAN MAKE HIM HAPPY.
AND WHEN I CAN GET THAT SMILE...
...I WILL BE THE HAPPIEST PERSON.

YOUR SMILE...
...HAS THE POWER TO MOVE ME.
RAIMON!
WAIT!!
IF YOU MAKE ANOTHER MOVE...
...YOU'LL HAVE TO SAY GOODBYE TO YOUR CRYSTAL!!
So stop... Please?!
DO WHAT YOU WANT.
It's not mine.
Hey!!
THAT'S MY CRYSTAL YOU'RE TALKING ABOUT!!
AND THIS IS ME MAKING AN EXIT. GOODBYE.
He's a runner!
OH, ONE MORE THING! I SET A BOMB IN WILSONS' HOUSE.
WITH THE PUSH OF THE BUTTON, YOUR HOUSE IS ALL BUT GONE!!
WHAT?!
PUSH IT.
It's not my house.
DON'T YOU DARE!!
HE CAME PREPARED!!
NO...!

CUT THAT OUT!
Eh?!
GIVE IT BACK TO HER!!
You're a lady, so act like one!
THAT'S DANGEROUS! AREN'T YOU GOING TO STOP HER?!
YOU CAN'T MAKE HER STOP.
SHE CAN TAKE CARE OF HERSELF.
BESIDES, SEEING HER ENJOYING WHAT SHE'S DOING...
...IS GOOD ENOUGH FOR ME.
You sound like...
YOU SEEM TO KNOW EVERYTHING ABOUT HER.

GIVE ME THAT!
NO WAY! IT BELONGS TO ADY, YOU GREEDY MONSTER.
YOU LITTLE...!
GEEZ...
KOTOBUKI...
WATCH OUT, KOTOBUKI!!
thud
TAKE...

...INITIATIVE.
KOTOBUKI, ARE YOU HURT?!
YOU HAVE BEEN WARNED.
CLICK
AHHHH!!
COME ON, KOTOBUKI. LET'S GO.
FORGET IT. YOU WON'T MAKE IT TO THE WILSON HOUSE.
Not in 30 seconds.
YOU MEAN...
...THE BOMB I REMOVED THE OTHER DAY?

IT ALWAYS ENDS WITH A BANG.
WHEN DID YOU NOTICE THE BOMB...?
...I...
HM?
I'LL START BY SAYING WHAT I ALWAYS WANTED TO TELL YOU.
IT'S YOU AND ME.
TOGETHER WE CAN MAKE IT WORK...
IF IT DOESN'T WORK, I'LL COME UP WITH SOMETHING ELSE.
LIKE MAKING TEA.
THANK YOU FOR THAT.
AND FOR TODAY.
ARE YOU TALKING TO ME?
Yes!!
IS IT THAT HARD TO TELL?!

YOU JUST WAIT, MOTHER!
I'm going right after it.
Sigh...
NO. I CAN'T...
MOTHER!!
WHAT'S WRONG?! STOP THAT!!
Kyaah!
ADY...
IT'S ALL RIGHT.
YOU CAN'T STOP ME ANYMORE.
I KNOW YOU'VE GOT ONE SCREW LOOSE, BUT LISTEN. I--
Now that's determination.

I...
MOTHER ...?
DO YOU HATE IT?
I'M GETTING BETTER...
I'VE SEEN A LOT WORSE.
But now you've seen it.
AH! I TOLD YOU NOT TO COME IN.
...
OH?!
I MESSED UP THE STITCHES, SO I THOUGHT I'D GIVE IT TO RAIMON INSTEAD, BUT HE DIDN'T WANT IT.
WHY WOULD I?
HOW...
...CONFUSING!!
That's life.

DID YOU USE THE OLD CALCULATOR? FATHER'S IS BROKEN.
The sleeves are different lengths.
IT'S STILL TOO BIG FOR YOU. YOU'LL GROW INTO IT, EVENTUALLY.
Oh! Ah!
I KNOW YOU STAY UP NIGHT AND STUDY.
YOU ARE NOT LIKE ME. I FEEL ASHAMED OF MYSELF.
I didn't know...
YOU'RE SO SMART, ADDY.
BUT I CAN TAKE CARE OF FINANCIAL MATTERS.
YOU CAN COUNT ON YOUR MOTHER!!
ADY?
OH?
OH?!
....

...
SHE'S TRYING, JUST WAY OFF.
I MUST HAVE LET YOU DOWN WITH THE DRESS...
がくっ
NO.
THIS IS...
...WHAT I WANTED...
THIS IS WHAT I'VE ALWAYS WANTED.
THIS IS THE ONE...
YOUR SMILE...

...HAS THE POWER TO MOVE ME.
KAMIHARA WAS ARRESTED.
What? He was a fraud? Oh, my.
ADY AND HER MOM SOLD THEIR BIG HOUSE.
And...
...YOU LOST YOUR JOB.
What a shame. You looked so cute.
......
IT'S OKAY.
Promise you'll write me when settled.
Promise.
I GOT ME A FRIEND.
PLUS THE SALARY! I'LL FIND ANOTHER JOB IN NO TIME!!
NONE FOR ME.
How come?

RAIMON...?
HM?
I...
I KNOW THIS ISN'T MUCH, BUT...
IT WILL GET US SOMETHING TO EAT...
SO... UM... YOU KNOW...
I'LL BUY YOU A MEAL!!
SO TELL ME WHAT YOU WANT TO EAT!!
There, I said it!!
KOTOBUKI.
FORGET IT.
I WANT TO EAT AN OMELET.
AN OMELET.

OKAY...!!
THAT CAN BE ARRANGED!!
HURRY, HURRY!!
I DIDN'T KNOW YOU LIKED OMELETS.
IT'S MY FAVORITE, TOO.
Let's tuck in.
YEAH.
MOTHER, I CAN'T GET KOTOBUKI'S IMAGE OUT OF MY HEAD...
WHAT'S WRONG WITH ME?
Oh, my.
THAT'S LOVE, ADY. LOVE.
My girl is suddenly grown up.
Wait, mom.

Welcome to the World of Tsubasa!
By the way, I have a cheongsam like this, but I haven't worn it yet. I wonder why I bought it...
Anyhoo, let's go.

翼を持つ者
つばさ も もの

The Extra (One) ← Not a very catchy title.

In the land of dreams.

EARTH IN THE 22ND CENTURY...
I'M SURE. IT'S RAIMON SHIRAGI.
...RIGHT. I WASN'T EXPECTING...
SIR, WE HAVE A NOTE ON THE GIRL FROM "F".
RAIMON TRAVELING WITH SOMEONE IS INTERESTING ENOUGH.
THIS IS EVEN BETTER.
KLAK
——...

THE THIEF KOTOBUKI...
RAAAIMON!
LOOK.
IT'S THE SEA!
YOU'VE NEVER SEEN IT BEFORE?
NOPE! CAN WE CAN GO IN?
I THINK IT'S STILL POLLUTED.
POLLUTED?!

FIELDS AREN'T THE ONLY THINGS THAT GOT HIT HARD DURING THE WARS.
HMM...
I'M HUNGRY.
WANNA GRAB SOMETHING IN TOWN?
UM...
BUT... YOU'RE GOING TO PAY AGAIN...
DON'T WORRY ABOUT IT.
JUST GIVE UP. YOU'LL NEVER BE RICH.
Not a chance.
Happy now?
Maybe you're right.
HOLD ON.
I HAVE AN IDEA.
YEAH?
LOOK. WE'VE BEEN ON THE ROAD FOR SOME TIME AND WE'RE STARVED. WE REALLY COULD USE YOUR HELP. A WALLET WILL DO--
THAT'S YOUR IDEA?!
THERE WERE SO MANY WARS...

BY THE START OF THE 22ND CENTURY, THE FIELDS WERE WITHERED AND THE EARTH WAS IN A STATE OF DESOLATION.
ONLY THE RICH, THE ARMY, AND THE POLITICIANS HAVE ACCESS TO THE NICER AMENITIES.
MEANWHILE, ORDINARY PEOPLE SUFFER IN POVERTY AND CRIME IS COMMON.
I WAS A THIEF IN ORDER TO SURVIVE, BUT IT'S ALL BEHIND ME NOW.
I'M TRAVELING FROM TOWN TO TOWN, LOOKING FOR A JOB.
WOULD YOU HIRE ME?!
NO GIRLS, BUT WE MIGHT NEED A GUY. WHAT DO YOU SAY, BUDDY?
Well
I'M SICKLY...
...AND WEAK.
AND I ONLY MAKE MYSELF USEFUL FOR KOTOBUKI.
I COULD DO A 100 TIMES BETTER THAN HIM!!
How about that?!
SORRY, NOT INTERESTED.
RAIMON SHIRAGI USED TO BE AN ELITE MILITARY OFFICER.

THE ARMY IS THE PLACE ONLY FOR THE PRIVILEGED FEW...
...AND RAIMON WAS A YOUNG CAPTAIN WITH A PROMISING CAREER.
HE HAS A TATTOO ON HIS LEFT CHEST TO PROVE IT.
HE KIND OF CHASED AFTER ME WHEN I WAS A THIEF...
...BUT HE QUIT THE ARMY SO WE COULD BE TOGETHER.
WE'VE BEEN TRAVELING TOGETHER FOR FIVE MONTHS, NOW.
I WANT TO BE GOOD ENOUGH FOR RAIMON, SOMEDAY.
SO HE CAN COUNT ON ME.
IN ORDER TO DO SO, I HAVE TO FIND HONEST WORK.
BUT...
I NEVER THOUGHT GETTING A JOB WAS SO DIFFICULT!!
Can jobs even play hard to get?!

Want a fish cake?
RELAX AND ENJOY YOUR MEAL.
BUT YOU'RE PAYING AGAIN...
With ※clean money, fortunately.
She stopped him earlier
YOU CAN DEPEND ON ME.
If we work together, robbing could be fun.
....
YOU DON'T NEED TO TRY SO HARD.
STOP FIGHTING IT.
Wh--
WHAT THE--!!
WHAT IS HE SAYING?
Stop that!
STOP MANIPULATING ME TO SUIT YOUR NEEDS!!
Grr!
I'm not joking.
Oh!
IS THAT ANY WAY TO TREAT YOUR LOVER?
PAT

WE SHOULD DO SOMETHING ABOUT YOUR WANDERING HAND.
I couldn't resist.
FEEL FREE TO TOUCH ME ANYWHERE, IN RETURN. ♡ ♡
ぎりぎりぎりぎりぎり
WORD HAS IT THAT TSUBASA ONCE LANDED HERE.
IN YOUR DREAMS!!
OUCH, THAT HURT.
Now I'm sad.
Ahhh!!
THIS LAND USED TO BE FERTILE...
LET'S BLAME THE HARD TIMES!!
Blame the poverty.
REALLY...?
TSUBASA IS A MYTH OF OUR TIME.
SOME PEOPLE BELIEVE THAT IT'S HIDDEN AND THAT WHOEVER FINDS IT WILL HAVE A WISH GRANTED.
Wow...
IT'S SAID TO HAVE SHOWN UP ONE DAY, AND THEN VANISHED AFTER GRANTING EVERYONE'S WISHES.
SOUNDS LIKE A MYSTERIOUS PLACE.
You think?

THIEF!!
WHO IS IT?!
I nearly had a heart attack!!
Ah ha ha!
EAT THIS!!
IT WASN'T ME!
RELAX, KOTOBUKI.
Poor girl...
!!
Klaaah!
..........!!

A CHILD...!!
KOTOBUKI!...
LET'S GO.
YEAH.
MY CHILD...
MY CHILD...
Huh?
W-WAIT!!
Mama!
KONG
OUCH!
COME ON!!
HURRY!!

ARE YOU HURT?
NO...
AIRA...
THEY LEFT...
...SOME-THING BEHIND...
!
STAY OUT OF IT.
I KNOW!
THEY CAN'T BE ON THE ROOF...
SMOOCH
GEEZ...
THEY'RE ALREADY GONE.

......
Oh!
MY BAD.
I'M IN A HURRY.
Sorry!
WHA--
WHAT JUST HAPPENED?!

I CAN'T THANK YOU ENOUGH...
I DIDN'T DO ANYTHING.
I didn't even try.
THANK THE LADY OVER THERE. THE ONE WHO KEEPS BRUSHING HER TEETH...
Sniff
Sniff
Sniff
THANK YOU SO MUCH.
WHAT'S WRONG?
NOZING NOZING.
*Nothing nothing.
IT'S OKAY. ANYWAY, WHAT'S UP WITH THEM?!
THEY'RE A RESISTANCE FORCE CALLED THE TEKI. YOU CAN TELL BY THE BANNER. THEY HAVE A HIDEOUT NEAR THE BEACH.
RESISTANCE?
IT'S A GROUP OF PEOPLE WHO HAVE A THING AGAINST THE MILITARY REGIME.
HM...

THEY STARTED TO RESORT TO VIOLENCE ABOUT A WEEK AGO...
...TO GET THE MESSAGE OUT
......
THE WORLD HAS GONE THOUGH A BIG CHANGE SINCE THE 21ST CENTURY, BUT THIS MAP WOULD SUFFICE.
THIS IS OUR COUNTRY, KNEELS.
DUVENI AND SOME OTHER SMALL COUNTRIES ARE RUN BY MILITARY, TOO.
*I improvised.
I GUESS NO COUNTRY IS WITHOUT A RESISTANCE.
THE ARMY USUALLY CALLS THEM "BLUE ROSE."
IT MEANS "NOT POSSIBLE."
......

THIS IS ONE OF THOSE TIMES WHERE I'M REMINDED THAT HE WAS IN THE ARMY.
...ARE THEY GONNA STOP THEM?
DON'T WORRY ABOUT THE ARMY.
THEY'RE NO STRANGER TO FOUL PLAY.
I WASN'T PART OF HIS LIFE BACK THEN.
SO WE'RE GOING TO SIT AROUND AND DO NOTHING?
NOT FOR NOW. THEY'RE EASILY PROVOKED. THE GROUP'LL CRY MILITARY BRUTALITY UNLESS THE ARMY HAS SOMETHING SOLID ON THEM.
Duveni is another story.
......?
Wait.
CAN I ERASE THE MAP?
NOT JUST YET.
I'VE NEVER SEEN A WORLD MAP BEFORE. IT'S AMAZING.
THE WORLD IS SO BIG.

THE WORLD IS SO BIG, AND I'M JUST A TINY DROP IN THE BUCKET.
Hmm...
DO YOU HAVE ANY PLANS FOR JOB HUNTING TOMORROW?
TEKI'S WREAKING HAVOC WITH THE TOWN...
OH, SHOOT. I STILL HAVE THAT BANNER.
......
I'LL GET RID OF IT.
I'm using your lighter.
WHAT WERE YOU BRUSHING YOUR TEETH FOR?
I'M JUST GOING TO GO AND SET IT ON FIRE.
ぴゅっ
......
I DIDN'T DO IT ON PURPOSE!!
IT WAS AN ACCIDENT. IT JUST HAPPENED!!

BUT...
...I STILL KISSED SOMEONE OTHER THAN RAIMON.
HE'S GOING TO HATE ME WHEN HE FINDS OUT!!
NOOO...
HEY!!
WHAT ARE YOU BURNING OUT HERE?
OH....
...MY GOD!

OFFICERS!!
WHAT HAVE WE GOT HERE?
Has a habit of running at the drop of a hat. →
THIS...
YOU'RE...
He put out the fire with his foot.
ARE YOU A MEMBER OF TEKI?
WHAT?!
NO WAY!!
I HEARD YOU MADE QUITE A SCENE TODAY.
TAKE HER.
WAI--
WAIT A MINUTE!!
YOU GOT IT ALL WRONG!! I FOUND IT ON THE STREET!!
RESISTING ARREST...
THAT LEAVES ME WITH NO CHOICE.

Ka-chak
OUCH--!
DON'T WORRY. IT'S NOT POISON.
IT'LL JUST MAKE YOU A BIT SLEEPY AND URGES YOU TO TALK.
HEY!!
HANDS OFF.

RAI...
Hey...!
WHAT ARE YOU--?! GET OFF!!
I COULD...
...EASILY...
...SHAKE HIM...
...OFF.

YOU'RE SAFE NOW...
pat
WH--
WHAT'S THIS?
I DID!!
NOW DON'T MAKE THIS ANY HARDER!!
Now.
WHO SHOT HER?
No drug works on Raimon.
SHE'S MINE.
STAY CLEAR, GOT IT?

ビクッ
CAPTAIN...
I DON'T HEAR A "YES, SIR."
WHAT'S WRONG WITH ME...?
......?
SHI--
CAPTAIN SHIRAGI...?!
YOU CAN LET HIM GO...
...RAIMON.

Sigh...
HERE COMES MAJOR TOYA INGRAM.
MA... JOR?
A POSITION MUCH ABOVE CAPTAIN.
WHAT?!
WHAT BRINGS HIM DOWN HERE...?
LONG TIME NO SEE.
RAIMON...
THIS IS A NEW LOW...
...EVEN FOR YOU, TOYA.
LOOK WHO'S TALKING.
Yikes.
First name basis?!

THE GIRL YOU TOOK UNDER YOUR WING IS LISTED AS A THIEF IN F'S DATABASE.
FROM WHAT I HEAR, SHE'S A MEMBER OF TEKI.
*F is the Army's mother computer.
Listen!
I'M NOT A MEMBER! ALTHOUGH THE THIEF PART IS TRUE...
カタ
カタ
カタ
カタ
ピ
NO.2416: DATA ON KOTOBUKI CLEARED.
Oh.
I ALMOST FORGOT.
HOW STUPID.
OH?! CAPTAIN SHIRAGI?!
LET GO.
I FORGOT TO ERASE IT.
HOW COULD YOU DO THAT, CAPTAIN SHIRAGI?!!
....
Sigh...
GEEZ... YOU MANIPULATE F SO EASILY, RAIMON.

YOU HAVEN'T CHAN--
IF YOU'RE TRYING TO GET ME THROUGH KOTOBUKI, YOU'D BETTER THINK AGAIN.
Heh heh...
IT'S PART OF MY JOB.
WE'VE BEEN KEEPING AN EYE ON TEKI. THEY'VE BEEN ACTING UP A LOT, LATELY.
......
...I GUESS YOU STILL HATE IT WHEN SOMEONE TOUCHES YOUR HAIR.
......
YOUR GIRL IS STILL A SUSPECT AS A MEMBER OF TEKI.
I SAID I AM NOT!!
Did you hear me?!
GO UNDERCOVER INTO TEKI AS A MOLE.
HOW DOES THAT SOUND?
HUH?
CONVINCE ME, YOUNG LADY. GIVE US SOMETHING TO WORK WITH.
SAY...
ARE YOU DEAF?!

TOYA!
SORRY, RAIMON. COMES WITH THE TERRITORY.
mumble
YOU KISSED ANOTHER GUY, DIDN'T YOU?
SO?
BUT I DON'T WANT TO BE A SPY...
Oh...
THAT'S RIGHT...
GIVE ME MORE DETAILS!!
Over there!
SORRY, RAIMON.
H-h-how...
HOW DID YOU KNOW THAT?!
I WAS PASSING.
STUPID. IT'S JUST MY WORD AGAINST YOU.

がくっ
...
WHY DIDN'T I THINK OF THAT...?
RAIMON WAS...
...LIKE A FLOWER TO THE COLONEL AND ME.
OH?
HE WAS OUR JOY. SEEING HIM GROW EACH DAY.
HE ALWAYS HAD A CHIP ON THE SHOULDER. I ADORED HIM.
Heh...
THESE ARE HIS PHOTOS FROM HIS CHILDHOOD. OH! HE HAD SUCH LOVABLE GLARE.
HE'S A BIT OFF...
BUT YOU CAME ALONG AND BROKE THE FLOWER.
キッ
No photos for you.
NOW YOU'VE LOST ME...
Oh, well.
IF I HADN'T DEPORTED HIM...
...HE WOULD HAVE MADE A FINE LIEUTENANT BY NOW.

LIEUTENANT...? I THOUGHT HE WAS ON THE POLICE FORCE FROM THE GET-GO.
I TAKE IT YOU DON'T KNOW MUCH ABOUT RAIMON AS AN OFFICER.
ZSSH
HOW SAD. AND YOU CLAIM TO BE HIS LOVER?
RAIMON'S?
LET ME BE STRAIGHT WITH YOU. I DON'T LIKE YOU.
...
NOW, TEKI HAS STARTED ROBBING ALL OVER THE TOWN.
I'D LIKE FOR YOU TO HELP US NAIL THEM. GET US SOMETHING GOOD.
I WILL GET RAIMON BACK.
IF YOU FAIL, I'LL TELL HIM ABOUT THE KISS...
...and have you arrested.
AND...
NOOOO!

...WELL?
B--
BASTARD!!
BRING IT ON.
YOU JUST WATCH.
GOOD. TEKI'S BASE IS BEHIND A CRAG NEAR THE BEACH.
THIS IS THE MAP. YOU WILL HAVE TO FIND YOUR OWN WAY IN, WITHOUT ANY HELP FROM RAIMON.
YOU DON'T HAVE TO TELL ME!
IF YOU SUCCEED, I'LL LET YOU KNOW EVERYTHING THERE IS TO KNOW ABOUT RAIMON.
STARTING WITH MY PRIVATE DIARIES.
All 20 volumes.
GET LOST.
Heh heh...
GOOD LUCK.

FOR YOUR INNOCENCE.
FOR RAIMON.
SO THE ARMY...
...HAS UNFINISHED BUSINESS WITH RAIMON...
TOYA WAS DEAD SERIOUS.
HE WANTS RAIMON BACK SO BADLY...
MY INNOCENCE?
THAT'S NOT MY PRIORITY!!
I'M NOT GOING TO...
...HAND HIM OVER!!
HAND OVER WHO?
N--
NOTHING.
Meow!
SO WHAT DID TOYA WANT? ARE YOU REALLY GOING UNDERCOVER?
Um?
YEAH... I GUESS.
Clear my name once and for all.

OKAY...
STAY OUT OF THIS. THIS IS MY PROBLEM, NOT YOURS...
IT'S ALL RIGHT.
I AM NOT GOING ANYWHERE.
I KNOW...
I WON'T...
I WON'T LET THEM TAKE HIM AWAY.
I GET IT. I'LL STAY ON THE SIDELINES.
JUST RE-MEMBER...
YOU DON'T HAVE TO HIDE ANYTHING FROM ME.

UNDERSTAND?
YOUR NECK IS SO THIN...
SUCH BIG...
...HANDS.

UGGGH!
Ouch...
WHY?!
I'M GOING FOR A WALK!!
どあーっ
WHY, WHY, WHY?!
WHY DID I...
...START SHAKING?!
HOW COULD I BE SO NAÏVE?
IT'S NATURAL.

RAIMON IS A MAN.
BUT...JUST THINKING ABOUT HIM MAKES MY KNEES GO WEAK.
ARE YOU SURE ABOUT KOTOBUKI...?
WELL, OUR ASSIGNMENT IS TO BUST TEKI AND FIND THAT THING.
ARE YOU READY FOR THIS?
MAJOR INGRAM...
YAN MIZUCHI...
THE HEAD OF TEKI.

The Extra (Two)
YAN, SOME OF THE FANS THINK YOU HAVE THE HOTS FOR KOTOBUKI.
HUH?!
How come?!
ゆらあ
……
IT'S NOT TRUE! THEY'RE WRONG! CALM DOWN!!
SHOKA!!
Don't run away!!

翼(つばさ)を持(も)つ者(もの)

MAJOR...
WE HAVE RECEIVED SOME FOX FROM THE HEADQUARTERS.
GOOD.
LET'S GET THIS SHOW ON THE ROAD.
IT WASN'T LIKE THIS BEFORE.
WE'D FOOL AROUND, BUT IT NEVER MADE ME SELF-CONSCIOUS.
HE CAN DO ANYTHING, AND HE'S SMART.
I THOUGHT OUR DIFFERENCES STOPPED THERE.

BUT NOW THAT I'VE REALLY LOOKED... HE'S A MAN.
KOH, THE FORMER HEAD OF TEKI, DIED TWO MONTHS AGO.
HIS SON, YAN MIZUCHI, TOOK OVER. THE GANG HAS 50 MEMBERS.
はあぁ
THAT'S ABOUT IT.
Huh?!
OH, RIGHT!!
CRAP! I'VE GOT TO FOCUS ON BUSINESS AT HAND!!
Wow...
THIS IS A DANGEROUS PLACE TO BUILD A HIDEOUT.
Base
SO ARE YOU GOING TO SNEAK IN?
I'M STILL THINKING... YOU SAID YOU'D STAY OUT OF THIS, REMEMBER?

I DID?
YES! DON'T PLAY DUMB!!
I AM TO INVESTIGATE WITHOUT ANY HELP FROM RAIMON.
THAT WAS THE PROMISE I MADE WITH TOYA.
TO CLEAR MY NAME AS AN ACCOMPLICE OF TEKI...
...AND, MORE IMPORTANTLY...
"IF YOU FAIL, I WILL TAKE RAIMON BACK."
...TO KEEP HIM AWAY FROM RAIMON!!
Grrrr!
KOTOBUKI, LISTEN.
I PROMISE I WON'T DO ANYTHING. SO CAN I STAY, PLEASE?
IF I CAN'T...
...I'LL GO OUT OF MY MIND.

THAT DEEP VOICE...
EARTH TO KOTOBUKI.
THOSE HANDS...
THAT BODY...
THE STRENGTH...
HE'S SO DIFFERENT FROM ME!!
WHY ARE YOU ALL BUNDLED UP?
Aren't you hot?
I CAN'T TELL HIM I FEEL SHY.
OH, THIS? I-IT'S NOTING
odd pose

WAIT.

SOMEONE'S COMING.

OH.

Kyaaah!

THE SHAKING HAS STARTED AGAIN!!

HOW COULD I OT FEEL NYTHING EFORE?

IT SEEMS IMPOSSIBLE THAT HE'S EVEN KISSED ME ALREADY.

F HE KISSES ME NOW...

...I'LL EXPLODE!!

WHAT?!

I WAS HOPING WE COULD GET THEM TO TALK AND GET IT OUT OF THE WAY QUICKLY.

THEY'RE NOT HERE. THOSE TWO GUYS WE SAW IN TOWN YESTERDAY.

They're gone.

I CAN SEE ONLY A FEW OF THEM.

MAYBE THEY'RE OUT ROBBING...

MAYBE.

....
There're things to do before going in.
...I'LL GO BACK TO TOWN...
YEAH...
....
ANYWAY...
HOW AM I GOING TO PROTECT RAIMON LIKE THIS...?
GOTCHA.
I'LL JUST GO AND LOOK AFTER SOMETHING...
Phew...
Wants it.

Clothes
WHAT A CUTE DRESS...
I'M JUST CURIOUS...
Eh heh...
DEFINITELY NOT ME...
I'VE NEVER WORN A DRESS LIKE THAT...
YOU LOOK LOVELY.
WHAT?!
I'VE NEVER SEEN YOU WEARING THAT KIND OF DRESS.
Ahh... Um...
YOU'LL LOOK GREAT IN IT. YOU'RE ALREADY PRETTY.
N- NO.
I'M GOING CRAZY...

...AND IT'S GETTING WORSE!!
HELLO...
...TO BOTH OF YOU.
Yikes!
TOYA!!
EASY, BOY.
WANNA HAVE A MEAL WITH ME?
JUST A MEAL...?
Heh...
OF COURSE.
YOUR FACE SAYS...
..."FOR NOW," YOU JERK.

WHAT'S WITH HIM...?
Oops.
MY BAD...
!!
WHAT AN ODD SCENT...
AH!
OH...
YOU AGAIN.
IT'S YOU...
...FROM YESTERDAY!
チュ
Yesterday
Ah ha ha!
IT WAS A CLOSE CALL, WASN'T IT? WE ALMOST KISSED.

DON'T WORRY ABOUT IT. WE SHARE THE SAME PAIN.
HEY...
NEXT TIME, LOOK WHERE YOU'RE GOING.
Bye!!
WAI-
Hold on a sec!
YOUR... GIVE ME YOUR NAME!!

YAN!
HEY. HOW'S IT GOING?
TOO EARLY TO TELL...
BUT I KNOW WE'LL OUTSMART THEM...
I CAN BET YOU THAT.
DON'T THEY HAVE MORE IMPORTANT THINGS TO DO THAN GOING AFTER US?
SLACKERS.

SO...
HOW'S YOUR INVESTIGATION GOING, KOTOBUKI?
I JUST STARTED. NOT MUCH I CAN DO IN ONE DAY.
OH DEAR. DON'T MAKE ME ARREST YOU...
Sigh...
I FEEL SORRY FOR THOSE GUYS IN TEKI.
The Army is full of jerks.
YOU DON'T KNOW WHAT YOU'RE SAYING.
Heh heh...
HAVE YOU SEEN THE SEA HERE?
LIFELESS OCEAN THAT LIGHT DOES NOT PENETRATE.
THAT'S THE RESULT OF HUMAN BEINGS TIPPING THE BALANCE AND TRYING TO RUN THE PLANET.
IT BEARS A SIMILARITY TO WHAT BLUE ROSE STANDS FOR.

THIS COUNTRY WOULD FALL APART WITHOUT THE ARMY.
WHAT ELSE CAN KEEP IT TOGETHER?
IT WOULDN'T LAST A YEAR.
TO LOOK FOR CHANGE MEANS...
...DESTROYING THE PEACE.
CHANGE...
"CHANGE"...
ドキン
BY THE WAY...
HOW FAR HAVE YOU TWO GONE?

なっ
What?!
...old goat.
NAUGHTY ...
Don't point your finger at me, son.
I WAS JUST CURIOUS.
Really.
IT DIDN'T MATTER...
IT DIDN'T MATTER...
...BE...
...FORE.
WHAT IS IT TO YOU?
I-IT'S--
......
LEAVE ME ALONE!!
ガタ
KOTOBUKI.
I'VE CHANGED.
MY FEELINGS FOR RAIMON ARE CHANGING...

KOTOBUKI.
...IN A VERY STRANGE WAY!!
NO...!
OH...
I--
I'M SORRY...
I'M SO... SORRY...

SORRY...
I COULD DIE.
I HURT HIM...!!
...
I DON'T GET IT, RAIMON...
WHAT DO YOU SEE IN HER?
SHE'S JUST A CHILD. SHE CAN'T HELP BUT PLAY GAMES.
...YES.
HM?

SHE'S SO CUTE I COULD JUST DIE...
"No!"
SHE'S SO INEXPERIENCED.
Not pleased.
......
SHE HASN'T HAD A CHANCE TO LEARN THE THINGS YOU DO WHILE GROWING UP.
SHE GREW UP ALONE.
THAT'S WHY SHE'S SO NAÏVE.
BUT...
I'M GOING TO TURN HER INTO A WOMAN.
......
THERE'S A CALMNESS IN YOUR EYES...
THE EMPTINESS I USED TO SEE IN THEM IS GONE.

I MISS THOSE EYES...
I WONDER HOW SHE'D FEEL IF SHE KNEW ABOUT THE OLD YOU.
GO AHEAD AND TELL HER.
RAIMON...
BYE.
......
THIS IS WHERE OUR DREAM LIVES...
sniff
sniff
sniff

I HURT HIS FEELINGS. WHAT DID I HIT HIM FOR?
I'M GOING THROUGH A CHANGE.
"TO LOOK FOR CHANGE MEANS DESTROYING THE PEACE."
IS THIS...
...THE END OF OUR RELATIONSHIP?
NO... PLEASE NO...
MAYBE IT IS. I CAN'T ACT CASUAL AROUND HIM ANYMORE.
HAVE I CHANGED BECAUSE I WANTED ALL OF THIS TO END?
WHY...?
WHAT DOES TEKI WANT TO CHANGE BY DESTROYING...
...WHAT WE HAVE?
ぴっ
WHAT WAS...?

ぴた
......
NOW THEY'VE DONE IT...
No finesse...
ゴオオ
Kyaaaah!
ワアアア
IT'S TEKI...!
THEY'VE DONE IT AGAIN!!
ワアア
IT'S ON FIRE...
WHY...
...DESTROY WHAT WE HAVE?
I HAVE TO...
...PUT OUT THE FIRE...
た

A BOMB?!
Oh--
OH MY GOD...
BACK OFF.
YO.
Ah!
IT'S YOU...!
WHY ARE YOU HERE...?
PING
GOOD. THIS ISN'T A REMOTE-CONTROL BOMB.
THE UPPER SIDE OF IT LOOKS PRETTY OLD-FASHIONED.
YAN!

WHAT?!
I'M GLAD I CAUGHT YOU. WE NEED YOUR HELP. WHAT'S THAT?
YAN? IS HE THE HEAD OF TEKI?!
SHE FOUND IT.
BUT.. HE'S BARELY OLDER THAN ME...
MAN, THEY'VE GOT SOME SERIOUS ISSUES.
Now, move!
GET THE OTHERS OUT OF HERE!
SOME OF YOU STAY TO PUT OUT THE FIRE!
THE REST COMB THE AREA, SEE IF THERE'RE OTHER BOMBS! IF YOU THINK YOU'RE IN REAL DANGER, RUN FOR YOUR LIFE!
OH?!
GO! NOW!
バタバタ
COPY THAT.
SO IT WASN'T THEIR DOING...
OH!

THAT NEW EXPLOSIVE, FOX, HAS SUCH AN AWFUL SMELL.
I HOPE THEY PLAN ON FIXING THAT.
It ruined my leather gloves
WHA--?
IT SMELLS FAMILIAR...
WHAT IS IT?
THAT'S RIGHT...
I GOT A WHIFF OF IT THE OTHER DAY ON ONE OF TOYA'S MEN...
?!
NEITHER OF YOU MOVE.
YAN, HEAD OF TEKI, AND KOTOBUKI...
...YOU ARE UNDER ARREST.

I'M CHARGING YOU WITH BURGLARY AND ATTACKS AGAINST THE ARMY THAT GO BEYOND THE BOUNDS OF A RESISTANCE.
WE HAVE ENOUGH EVIDENCE, NOW.
TOYA...
I KNEW YOU WERE UP TO SOMETHING...
?!
がばっ
BURGLARY? YOU PUT YOUR BOYS UP TO IT!
I WAS RIGHT. IT'S THE SAME SMELL...
YOU'VE HAD...
...THE WHOLE THING PLANNED FROM DAY ONE!!
HE...
HE PLAYED ME!!
YOU LOST.
Dammit!

ガリ ガリ
Second generation always gets the short end of the stick.
THIS IS WHY I DIDN'T WANT TO TAKE OVER THE GANG.
BUT I THOUGHT I'D RUN IT MY WAY WITHOUT KNOWING WHAT MY WAY WOULD BE.
WELL, ENOUGH WHINING.
EMOTION NEVER STAYS STILL. IT CONSTANTLY EVOLVES.
I didn't mean it.
Ah!
WHY DID I CHANGE MY MIND?
Y-
YAN?
EVOLVE...
?!
tic
tic
WHAT ARE YOU GOING TO DO WITH YAN?
YAN!!
You idiot...
YOU HAVEN'T STOPPED THE BOMB!!

HUH?!
GET RID OF IT...!
AH?!
RAI...!
plink

WOW...
LOOKING GOOD, RAIMON.
THEY'RE ALL GONE, SIR!
GO AFTER THEM. YOU MAY USE FORCE, BUT DON'T HURT RAIMON.
ARE YOU OKAY?
YEAH, RUNNING ISN'T THAT BAD...
LOOK...
HM?
...I'M SORRY...
...I HIT YOU.
I'M SORRY...
THEN KISS ME.

OH.
YOU NEVER KISS ME, KOTOBUKI.
DON'T MIND ME. PRETEND I'M NOT HERE.
Enjoy.
WHA--
Wha ?!
YAN!!

!!
......
SHE FELL...
WE'LL SEARCH FOR KOTOBUKI, JUST IN CASE.
BUT IN THAT POLLUTED WATER, WHAT ARE THE CHANCES...?

I DON'T GET IT. WHY DO YOU WANT TO DESTROY TEKI SO MUCH?
TSUBASA.
MANKIND'S DREAM...
THEY THINK IT MIGHT BE BELOW YOUR GROUP'S BASE.
?!
Tsubasa? Seriously?
WELL DONE. THAT, AND...
...TSUBASA HOLDS A SPECIAL MEANING TO THE ARMY. TO US.
RIGHT, RAIMON?
RAIMON?

翼を持つ者

Beep
NO SIGN OF HER?
NOT YET. BUT IN THAT DIRTY WATER...
...IT'S MOST LIKELY THAT...
...WE'VE LOST HER.
So...
YOU'RE SAYING OUR HOME IS...
...WHERE TSUBASA LANDED.
I had no idea.
Heh heh...
WE DETECTED SOME KIND OF MAGNETIC FIELD RUNNING BELOW THE BUILDING, AND WE BELIEVE IT TO BE TSUBASA.

OF COURSE WE DON'T EXPECT TO FIND TSUBASA ITSELF THERE...
...but there might be a clue.
RIGHT...
SO YOU WENT TO ALL THAT TROUBLE JUST TO DIG UP OUR HOME?
Heh heh...
IT WAS ABSOLUTELY NECESSARY, TSUBASA IS OUR ONLY HOPE.
TSUBASA WILL GIVE US THE POWER TO RUN THE WORLD WITHOUT THE WARS OTHERWISE NEEDED TO ACHIEVE IT.
BUT IF IT FALLS INTO THE HANDS OF OTHER COUNTRIES, IT POSES A REAL THREAT.
IF WE LAUNCH AN OFFICIAL SEARCH OF THE AREA, OTHER COUNTRIES WILL KNOW WHAT WE'RE UP TO AND DECLARE A WAR.
IT SOUNDS... COMPLICATED.
IS IT REALLY OKAY FOR THE ARMY TO BE DEPENDENT ON TSUBASA?
IF IT GIVES OUR COUNTRY THE POWER WE ASPIRE TO, YES.
WE'RE WILLING TO TAP INTO IT.

YOU MAKE IT SOUND LIKE IT'S A WEAPON.
I THOUGHT TSUBASA WAS...
...A MORE HOPEFUL THING.
Heh heh...
YAN, YOU CAN'T POSE A REAL THREAT. YOU JUST DON'T HAVE IT IN YOU.
......
TAKE HIM TO A CELL.
Oh!
RAIMON, I NEED TO APOLOGIZE...
KOTOBUKI AND I KISSED, ONCE.
SORRY ABOUT THA...
BANG

Come, now...
THAT'S HIS WAY OF SAYING SHUT UP.
Hurry up, or he won't miss next time.
DUDE...
YOU'RE DANGEROUS.
Ambidextrous.
TOYA.
RAIMON...
ROUND UP THE GROUP. WE'LL MAKE AN EXAMPLE OUT OF YAN IN FRONT OF THEM, AND WE'LL FINISH OFF THE REST LATER.
THAT WAY, WE CAN FOCUS ON THE DIGGING.
IF YOU'RE GOING TO EXECUTE YAN SOONER OR LATER...
...WHY NOT JUST MAKE IT TOMORROW AT NOON?
YOU'RE FINALLY...
...BACK WITH US.
OH, SORRY. I COULDN'T RESIST.
No touching the hair.

SO, HOW LONG DID YOU KNOW THAT WE HAD OUR EYES ON TSUBASA?
FROM THE MOMENT I SAW YOU, TOYA.
I'M SORRY ABOUT KOTOBUKI.
IT'S...
...FINE.
IT'S NOTHING.
I'M SO GLAD TO HAVE YOU BACK. WE'LL CONTINUE OUR QUEST FOR TSUBASA LIKE WE USED TO.
HE SEEMS LIKE A DIFFERENT MAN...
THAT'S THE RAIMON I KNOW.
PEOPLE USED TO REGARD HIM IN AWE.
HE CAN BE A HANDFUL, BUT I'M HAPPY TO HAVE HIM BACK ON BOARD.
AT LEAST KOTOBUKI'S DEATH CONTRIBUTED SOMETHING. IT'S NOT LIKE SHE WOULD HAVE EVER ADDED UP TO MUCH ALIVE.

SHE WAS TOO BORING...
I FEEL LIKE I'M BEING SUCKED IN...
NO... I DON'T WANT TO DIE JUST YET...
I WANTED TO PROTECT HIM...
BUT INSTEAD, I HIT HIM...
HE WAS SMILING, BUT WHAT IF HE THINKS...
...I HATE HIM...?
I CAN'T...
...MOVE...
WHAT IS...YOUR WISH?
WHAT IS...YOUR WISH ?
WHAT...?
MY WISH...?

I WANT TO...

...SEE RAIMON...

...EVEN THOUGH I MIGHT HURT HIM AGAIN...

WHY?

BECAUSE LATELY...

...IT'S BEEN WEIRD.

IT WASN'T LIKE THIS BEFORE.

IS THAT A GOOD OR A BAD THING?

"TO LOOK FOR CHANGE MEANS DESTROYING THE PEACE."

YOU'RE EVOLVING, THAT'S ALL.

YOU'RE EVOLVING FOR SOMEONE YOU CARE ABOUT.

EVOLVING...?

IT'S ALL RIGHT.

YES. IT'S NOT DESTROYING. YOU ARE GROWING.

SEE?

LIKE US.
THIS IS EVOLUTION.
IT'S GLOWING. IN THIS POLLUTED WATER...
NOW YOU WILL GET YOUR WISH.
THE REST IS UP TO YOU...
IT'S SO... BEAUTIFUL...

IT'S A LOVELY DAY FOR EXECUTION, ISN'T IT?
YAN!!
YAN!!
YOU SAID YOU WOULDN'T KILL HIM IF WE TURNED OURSELVES IN!!
I look lame.
SORRY, GUYS. THEY USED ME AS BAIT...
I'VE NEVER FELT SO STUPID.
DON'T WORRY. THEY'LL BE FOLLOWING YOU.
Huh?
DON'T MAKE IT ANY HARDER FOR ME.
FIRST THE GIRL, AND NOW MY BOYS? I FEEL WORTHLESS.

SO DO THE WORLD A FAVOR...
...AND FINISH ME OFF.
?!
Ugh...
I GOT SEAWATER ON ME...
...YOU...?
JUST GET IT OVER WITH, WHY DON'T...

UH...
W-wha--?!
SHE'S NOT DEAD?!
......
Yan...?
WHAT'S GOING ON?
YOU LOOK LIKE A PRISONER WAITING...
...TO BE EXECUT-ED...
すく
SOLDIERS...
Gyah?!

WHY ARE YOU EXECUTING HIM?!
Ahhhh!
BACK OFF!!
RAIMON...
THERE YOU ARE. THEY SHOULD BE DONE WITH THE EXECUTION BY NOW.
GATHER EVERYONE UP. WE HAVE SOME EXPLAINING TO DO.
YOU GOT IT.

THAT WAS CLOSE...
YOU OKAY, YAN?
Huff
Huff
Yan!
YOU TELL ME. ARE YOU OKAY? YOU DON'T FEEL SICK?
Thank goodness!
HOW DID YOU GET OUT OF THE WATER?
Huh?
Yan!
I-I JUST DID...
I HEARD A VOICE...
ABOVE AND BEYOND?
Wow.
IT WAS SO BEAUTIFUL... IT ASKED ME WHAT I WANTED...
RAIMON!
WHERE IS HE?!
Oh.
HE'S BACK IN THE ARMY.
Yan!
HUH?
TOYA FORCED HIM TO RETURN, RIGHT?!
UH... HE SEEMED FINE WITH IT, TO ME...

~yan
Yaan
ALTHOUGH HE'S DIFFERENT, NOW. HE'S SCARY...
NO... I CAN'T BELIEVE HE'D DO THAT...
SOMETHING MUST HAVE HAPPENED WHEN I WAS GONE!!
!
ZERO2のさくらら
Ugh!
QUIT WHINING. I'VE FORGOTTEN SOMETHING...
I WANT TO...
...PROTECT RAIMON, DON'T I?!
I'VE GOT TO SAVE RAIMON...!
GOT ANY PLANS?
Uh...
NOT YET...
BUT I WILL GET HIM OUT OF THERE.
HOW?
←Now freed:

?
WITH THE POWER OF LOVE!!
NOT THAT I'D EVER REALLY SAY THAT...
I DON'T KNOW IF HE GOT OVER IT.
I'VE GOT TO SEE HIM...
...AND TELL HIM THAT I LIKE HIM.
I'LL HELP YOU OUT.
OH?
YOU SAVED MY LIFE, AFTER ALL.
AND THE WAY YOU SHOWED UP WHEN EVERYONE THOUGHT YOU WERE DEAD...
...MAKES ME WANT TO TAKE MY CHANCES WITH YOU.
......?

Whoa!
ANOTHER EXPLOSION?!
IT'S NOT FROM TOWN. IT'S...
...OUR HIDE-OUT!!
GIVE ME A BREAK.
THE ROCKY HILL FELL BECAUSE OF THE EXPLOSION.
MAJOR, THE DOOR IS BLOCKED.
OH, DEAR... HOW'D THAT HAPPEN?
RAIMON, ARE YOU OKAY?

DON'T MOVE.
M002783E
RAIMON...
THAT WAS JUST A TEST. I SET DOZENS OF BOMBS IN THE MOUNTAIN. THEY'LL GO OFF IN FIVE MINUTES.
IT WAS YOU...
THIS HILL IS NOT VERY BIG.
I DON'T WANT TO DIE ALONE...
...SO YOU AND TSUBASA...
...ARE GOING TO SINK INTO THE SEA WITH ME.
HE'S BLUFFING, RIGHT?
No.
I DON'T THINK HE IS.

HE'S DONE THIS TWICE IN THE PAST.
THE FIRST TIME, HE AND SEVERAL OTHER OFFICERS WERE BADLY HURT.
WHEN ASKED WHY HE DID IT, HE SAID HE WAS BORED.
WHY ARE YOU DOING THIS...?
I DON'T WANT TO LIVE IF KOTOBUKI...
...ISN'T HERE.
KOTOBUKI?!
WHAT'S SO SPECIAL ABOUT HER?!
I TOLD YOU... KOTOBUKI WAS STILL IN THE MAKING.
SHE WAS ALWAYS SO FULL OF HOPE.
SHE WAS GROWING.

SHE WAS THE ONLY THING...
...THAT GAVE MEANING TO MY LIFE...
MAJOR!!
YOU RUINED IT...
...TOYA.
YOU...
YA!!
......
I TOLD YOU NOT TO MOVE...
...DIDN'T I?

HE CAN'T BE... STOPPED.
CAT GOT YOUR TONGUE, TOYA?
WHAT'S WRONG? ARE YOU AFRAID?
I'M JUST SAD THAT YOU'VE BETRAYED ME.
Heh...
...STUPID.
THIS IS THE REAL RAIMON.
ONCE HE SNAPS, THERE'S NO STOPPING HIM.
THERE'S NO ONE...
Ouch...
ガ

......
THERE YOU ARE...
KOTOBUKI ...?
?!
RAIMON, YOU'RE BLEEDING...!
Stop...!
DON'T! HE'S DANGERO--
WHAT'S UP WITH YOU, RAIMON...?

......!
I'M SORRY I MESSED UP... WERE YOU...
... WORRIED?
...YEAH.
ドキン
I LIKE HIM.
I LIKE HIM. I LIKE HIM SO MUCH.
I CAN SAY IT A HUNDRED TIMES OVER, BUT IT STILL WON'T BE ENOUGH.
JUST BEING... CLOSE TO HIM...
...IS NOT ENOUGH ANYMORE.
THAT'S HOW MUCH I LIKE HIM.

I WAS GOING THROUGH AN EVOLUTION.
IT TOOK ME A WHILE TO REALIZE...
...THAT I STARTED TO LIKE HIM...
...A LOT MORE THAN BEFORE.
THIS IS A FIRST...
YOU KISSED ME.
RIGHT?
ひょいっ
WHOA!
AH HA HA!
STOP THAT! YOU'RE SCARING ME.

YOU COULDN'T STAND BEING TOUCHED BY ME...
...BUT YOU'RE FINE WITH HER...
KOTOBUKI...
IT'S REALLY YOU...
YOU'RE NOT DEAD...
I'M GLAD I'VE NOTICED HIM.
BECAUSE IT...
...FEELS SO GOOD.
OH!
WE SHOULD GET OUT OF HERE...
...BEFORE THE BOMBS GO OFF.
Huh?

That's sudden.
LET'S GO... OH, AND YAN IS OUTSIDE.
......
SO WHAT HAPPENED TO COMMITTING SUICIDE, RAIMON?
LET'S RUN.
Huh?
WHAT SUICIDE?
NOW...
WHAAAT?!
Phew...
KOTOBUKI CLIMBED UP THE WINDOW AND TOOK OFF.
I HOPE SHE'S OKAY.
YAN!
THERE SHE IS...
THE CLIFF'S GONNA COLLAPSE!
RUN!!

EH
IT'S GONNA EXPLODE!
Hurry up!
WHOA...
Huff
Huff
Huff
IT'S GOING DOWN...
Goodbye, home!
DID TOYA AND OTHERS MAKE IT OUT?
Everyone started running in all directions.
NO WORRIES.
OH?
WHAT'S THAT? SOMETHING'S SHINING...

OH....
I SAW THAT IN THE WATER...!!
MAYBE IT'S SEA ANEMONE...?
......
HMM...
HAVE A CLOSER LOOK, KOTOBUKI.
THE WATER RUNNING OVER IT IS CLEAR.
YEAH... IT IS.
NOW WE KNOW HOW YOU GOT OUT OF THE WATER FINE.
IT'S CLEANING THE POLLUTED WATER OF THE SEA.
THAT WASN'T HERE BEFORE.
I GUESS IT EVOLVED...

... KOTOBUKI.
SO IT'S ALL RIGHT...
...TO TAKE YOUR TIME, TOO...
IN THE POLLUTED WATER...
...IT GREW UP LITTLE BY LITTLE...
"LIKE US."
IT SEEMS LIKE...
......
...RAIMON KNEW EVERYTHING...
...THE WHOLE TIME.
HEY...
UH... WHAT'S THAT?
HM?

ぱあっ
?!
YOUR WISH...
THAT VOICE...!!
...CAME TRUE.
WHAT...
...WAS THAT...?
I'M VERY HAPPY FOR YOU.
THAT'S GOOD.
......

COULD IT BE...
"WHAT IS YOUR WISH?"
TSUBASA?
YOU'VE GOTTA BE JOKING! I WANNA SEE IT AGAIN!
IT FLEW AWAY.
WHAAT?!
I...
I'M NOT SURE. BUT IT SAID SOMETHING ABOUT A WISH...
IT'S POSSIBLE.
"WHAT IS..."
"...YOUR WISH?"
OH, DEAR...
WE LOST TEKI, TSUBASA IS AT THE BOTTOM OF THE OCEAN...
...AND RAIMON FELL OFF THE RADAR AGAIN.
The colonel won't be pleased...

WE CAN SEND OUR FORCE...
NO, I'LL GIVE UP FOR NOW.
KOTOBUKI WON THIS TIME.
KOTOBUKI HAS...
SHE HAS... POTENTIAL.
AT LEAST SHE STOPPED RAIMON...
I'M SURE WE'LL SEE EACH OTHER AGAIN.
Until then, I'll keep my diaries.
What diaries?
IT WAS SO BEAUTIFUL...
IF A DREAM COULD HAVE A SHAPE, IT WOULD BE THAT.
SO, IN A NUT-SHELL...
...TSUBASA SAVED YOUR LIFE. TOYA WOULD BE HAPPY TO HEAR THAT.
He might experiment on your body.
NO WAY! I'D RATHER NOT SEE HIM AGAIN.

RAIMON...
DID YOU REALLY TRY TO KILL HIM?
YEP. HE KISSED YOU.
HE KNOWS!!
I-I'M SO SORRY!
IT WAS AN ACCIDENT! I KNOW THIS SOUNDS LAME, BUT...
UM...
I'LL FORGIVE YOU IF YOU KISS ME. ♡
KONG
じーん
WHY ARE YOU ALWAYS LIKE THAT?
Heh heh...
...I'LL HAVE TO WAIT A BIT LONGER TO MAKE YOU A WOMAN.
THE WORLD...
THE ARMY, TSUBASA, BORDERS...
...IS SO BIG.
ぴたっ

I'M GLAD...
...THAT THERE'S STILL SOMEONE LIKE YOU.
HUH?
It's just...
YOU MADE ME REALIZE THAT I NEED TO SEE MORE OF THE WORLD.
I NEED THAT TO KEEP RUNNING THE RESISTANCE...
THE WORLD IS FULL OF THINGS WAITING TO BE DISCOVERED.
YAN!
YO!
I'M GONNA GO. HAVE FUN WITH YOUR BOYFRIEND.
HE'S A DISASTER WAITING TO HAPPEN, AND YOU'RE THE ONLY ONE WHO CAN STOP HIM.
HE ALMOST KILLED ME, YOU KNOW.
I can hear you.
WHAT?!
HOPE TO SEE YOU AGAIN.
Bye!

...AND RAIMON...
SOMETIMES EVERYTHING SEEMS OVERWHELMING FOR ME, BUT--
BUT...
YANK
...YOU CAN EVOLVE.
Twirl
...LITTLE BY LITTLE...
ONE KISS...
...A DAY.
IT WAS FUN WATCHING YOU GET UPSET, THOUGH. ♡
YOU ARE SUCH A PIECE OF WORK.

TOYA, FANS WANT TO SEE YOUR PHOTO COLLECTION OF RAIMON.
HM?
NOT GONNA HAPPEN. THIS IS MY TREASURE YOU'RE TALKING ABOUT. IT'S PROOF OF MY LOVE. NOW YOU KNOW HOW I FEEL ABOUT YOU, RAIMON.
Oh, no!!
YOU WILL **NEVER** GET MARRIED...
Stay away.
I'M NOT THAT KEEN ON THE PHOTOS.
HE'S GOT A WIFE AND KIDS.
WHAT? IS SOMETHING WRONG?
NO WAY!!
A secret revealed!!

翼を持つ者

!!
FANS WANT TO SEE SOME ACTION BETWEEN RAIMON AND KOTOBUKI. SOME EVEN THINK RAIMON SHOULD THROW HIMSELF AT KOTOBUKI. ANY COMMENTS, GUYS?
WELL... MY PRIORITY IS KOTOBUKI, SO I DON'T WANT TO RUSH AND HURT HER FEELINGS.
IF I FORCE MYSELF ON HER, I'LL HURT HER FEELINGS. AND HAVING A RELATIONSHIP IS NOT ALL ABOUT SEX. BUT LET ME ASSURE YOU...
WHEN IT HAPPENS, IT HAPPENS.
じー
You seem ready.
DON'T SAY ANOTHER WORD...
AT LEAST THE READERS HAVE SOMETHING TO LOOK FORWARD TO.
Don't stare...
WHETHER OR NOT THERE'S MORE...
...is beyond our control.
Sigh...
THINKING THAT IS BAD LUCK!!
And with a sigh.

"GOOD LUCK TO ALL OF US."
"LET'S FIND OUR PROOF OF..."
"...LIFE."
THIEF!!
Four Seasons
YOU LITTLE DIRTBAG!! YOU ARE A NAMELESS ONE, AREN'T YOU?!
THE NAMELESS ONES ARE BETTER OFF DEAD!!

IT'S THE END OF THE 22ND CENTURY ON EARTH.
THERE WERE SO MANY WARS. THE FIELDS ARE WITHERED, AND ORDINARY PEOPLE SUFFER IN POVERTY.
BUT LIFE GOES ON, NO MATTER WHAT.
I'M KOTOBUKI. I USED TO BE A THIEF IN ORDER TO SURVIVE THE HARD TIMES...
THAT'S GOOD.
IT'S NICE OUT.

...BUT THAT'S ALL BEHIND ME, NOW.
I'VE BEEN TRAVELING FROM TOWN TO TOWN TO FIND AN HONEST JOB...
Morning!
LET'S WORK HARD, TODAY.
GOOD MORNING, KOTOBUKI!
OH!
...AND I FINALLY DID IT.
Yaay!
I GOT A JOB AT AN ORPHANAGE.
THE ORPHANAGE IS BUILT OUT OF A ROCKY MOUNTAIN.
I DO A LITTLE BIT OF EVERYTHING THERE.
KOTOBUKI.
Oh
GOOD MORNING, DIRECTOR.

THANK YOU FOR YOUR HARD WORK...
EVEN THOUGH WE'RE NOT PAYING YOU MUCH...
Don't be silly!
THIS IS MY CALLING.
Now...
TIME FOR LAUNDRY AND TIDYING-UP! I'LL GET THE WATER AND THEN I'LL COOK.
WHAT AN ENERGETIC CHILD...
It's as if she's sucking up my energy.
I'LL HELP YOU OUT.
OH.
I ALMOST FORGOT.
HAVE YOU SEEN RAIMON?
RAIMON?
HE WAS CLEANING UP THE LOUNGE.

RAIMON IS CLEANING UP?!
RAIMON!!
GOOD MORNING. ♡
W-WHAT'S GOING ON? WHAT ARE YOU DOING?!
And what's up with the broom?
I'M CLEANING.
W-WHY? WHAT FOR?
I JUST WANTED TO HELP YOU, KOTOBUKI.
TAP
THIS IS MY COMPANION, RAIMON SHIRAGI.
RAIMON WAS A YOUNG CAPTAIN WITH A BRIGHT FUTURE...
...BUT HE QUIT THE ARMY BECAUSE HE WANTED TO BE WITH ME.

WE'VE BEEN TRAVELING TOGETHER EVER SINCE.
Hee!
Yay!
COME ON, GUYS. WE SHOULD KEEP THOSE LOVEBIRDS ALONE.
Kotobuki!
WE'LL DO THE LAUNDRY.
HUH? WAIT!!
GOOD BOY.
... RAIMON ...
YOU DON'T HAVE TO GO TO THE TROUBLE TO DO ALL THIS...
WHEN I WAS A MAID, HE DIDN'T EVEN RAISE A FINGER.
Help needed at orphanage
BUT...
IT'S DIFFERENT THIS TIME.
THERE'S AN OPENING AT AN ORPHANAGE... I WANT TO CHECK IT OUT.
GO AHEAD.

I'LL START WORKING, TOO.
I'VE NEVER SEEN THIS SIDE OF HIM.
THE RAIMON I KNOW DOESN'T CARE ABOUT ANYONE AND TREATS EVERYONE LIKE DIRT.
ALTHOUGH HE LOOKS QUITE COMFORTABLE AROUND KIDS...
Oddly enough...
DON'T WORRY ABOUT ME. THIS IS A DREAM COME TRUE FOR YOU.
...YEAH.
MY DREAM WAS TO FIND WORK.
I WANTED TO QUIT ROBBING AND START A NEW LIFE. I WANTED TO STAND ON MY OWN TWO FEET.
GOOD LUCK.
smooch
THEN I'LL BELIEVE IN MYSELF.

IT'S A STEP TOWARDS BECOMING MORE LIKE SOMEONE WORTHY OF HIS ATTENTION.
Meow ...
mumble...
MY ONLY CONCERN IS THAT HIS SECOND HOUSE IS IN THIS TOWN...
MYA?
AND THERE'S THIS GUY...
IT'S NOTHING. ♡
OH!
WHAT'S WRONG?
SOMEBODY PLEASE HELP!!
SIS KOTOBUKI!
WE WENT TO TOWN FOR SHOPPING...

HERE.
YOU WANT IT, YOU TAKE IT.
HEY!!
STOP THAT! HE'S ONLY A CHILD!!
KOTOBUKI ...!
WHO ARE YOU?
A FRIEND OF THOSE NAMELESS ONES?
MOMMY, WHAT IS A NAMELESS ONE?

IT'S PEOPLE WHO DON'T HAVE A FAMILY. YOU BECOME A NAMELESS ONE...
...IF YOUR PARENTS DIE OR ABANDON YOU.
IF YOU DON'T HAVE A NAME, THEY WON'T ISSUE YOU IDENTIFICATION. THAT'S WHY THEY'RE CALLED NAMELESS ONES.
OH, YOU'RE THE WOMAN WHO'S STARTED WORKING IN THAT DUMP.
IT'S CALLED AN OR-PHANAGE.
IT'S NOT A WISE DECISION...
WELL, THE PRICES ARE SOARING.
YOU CAN'T EVEN BUY ONE BLOCK OF SUGAR.
OH, REALLY? THEN WE WANT OUR MONEY BACK.
THIS MONEY CAME FROM THE ARMY, RIGHT?
THEN IT'S OUR MONEY. WE PAY TAXES.
Idiot.
LET THEM EAT ROOTS. KEEPS THEM IN THEIR PLACE.
Ah ha ha!

YOU WANT IT BACK?
THEN COME AND GET IT!
AGH!
I GOT IT!
WHAT THE-- GIVE THAT BACK TO ME!
Bitch...
YOU TOLD ME TO GET IT, SO I DID...
YOU LITTLE...

KOTOBUKI!!
!
YOU'RE DEAD, YOU SCUM.
SNAP
GAAAAHHH!
NO VIOLENCE, PLEASE.
LET'S TALK.
YOU...!!
LET'S NOT GET ROUGH...
...on such a sweet lady.
RAIMON...
You took your time walking here.

SEE?
VIOLENCE BRINGS YOU NOTHING.
......

YOU DIDN'T HAVE TO DO THAT...
I NEED SOME GOOD EXERCISE.
......
Corpul
......
WHAT WAS THAT SOUND?!
?!
Oh, no!
IT'S THE ARMY AGAIN!!
RAIMON, WE'D BETTER RUN.
WHY?
Stupid!
THEY STILL WANT YOU BACK.
THEY'VE MADE THAT ABUNDANTLY CLEAR, REMEMBER?
THE ARMY HAS UNFINISHED BUSINESS WITH RAIMON.
THOUGH I DON'T KNOW WHAT MAKES HIM SO VALUABLE TO THEM.
Thanks for caring.
IT'LL BE FINE.

HE'S OUT OF IT. DID YOU HIT HIM?!
Huh?
THAT'S JUST STUPID.
I KICKED HIM.
YOU IDIOT!!
OF COURSE I DIDN'T HIT HIM.
HEY...
NICE GUN.
A CONVERTED GUN MANU-FACTURED BY CORPUL CORP.
It's his. Not mine.
WHA--

LET'S GO.
EH?!
But--
WE'RE FREE TO WALK.
...LET'S GET YOU HOME.
ギゅっ
"NAMELESS ONE"!!
WHAT'S THE PROBLEM?
OH, SIR, IT'S--
SIR, WE HAVE A SITUATION...
I SEE...

Hey!
FOR NOW, GIVE THE POOR GUY SOME TIME TO COOL OFF.
The poor guy.
YES, SIR...
...OH, DEAR.
カチ
WHO WOULD KNOW SOMETHING LIKE THAT...
...OTHER THAN HIM?
...OKAY.
TO TELL YOU THE TRUTH, IT'S NOT THE FIRST TIME WE'VE BEEN TREATED THAT WAY...
OF COURSE, THE ARMY HELPS US FINANCIALLY...
...BUT THEY DON'T GIVE US MUCH.

THANKS TO ROSS'S HELP...
...WE MANAGE WELL.
ROSS WHO?
A WEALTHY MAN WHO HAS BEEN SPONSORING US FOR DECADES.
HE HAS A LARGE SECOND HOUSE IN THIS TOWN.
I HAVE ONE WORRY, THOUGH.
THERE HAS BEEN A STRING OF ATTACKS AGAINST ORPHANAGES. SOMEONE'S ON A DESTROYING SPREE.
WHAT?! WHY?!
BUT WHY ORPHAN-AGES?
I DON'T THINK THEY'RE TARGETING US... IT'S JUST A WAY OF GETTING AT AUTHORITIES LIKE THE ARMY.
I DON'T KNOW.
PERHAPS THEY ARE WHAT YOU CALL BLUE ROSE.
Here's an article.

THE POOR CHILDREN. WHY DO THEY HAVE TO GO THROUGH SUCH MISERY?
NO FAMILY NAME, NO MEANS OF IDENTIFICATION... AND NO CHANCE AT EDUCATION.
SOME CHILDREN CAN'T EVEN GET INTO AN ORPHANAGE.
CAN I SEE THE ARTICLE?
OH... SURE.
DO YOU WANT A LOOK, TOO, KOTOBUKI?
......
...THANKS, BUT...
I CAN'T READ IT.
I can only write and read a few basic words.
TO TELL YOU THE TRUTH...
I'M A NAMELESS, TOO.

ぎゅっ
...OH MY.
OH...!!
I REALLY ADMIRE WHAT YOU DO, LADY, TAKING CARE OF ALL THOSE KIDS BY YOURSELF.
WE CAN DO THIS.
WE'RE IN THIS TOGETHER.
LET'S LIVE!
YES, SURE...
THAT'S A GOOD IDEA.
Anyway...
THIS IS A PRETTY BIG CASE.
THREE BLOWN UP BUILDINGS... A FEW DEAD BODIES...

すくっ
HOW CAN THE ARMY LET THEM COMMIT SUCH HORRIBLE ACTS AND NOT DO ANYTHING?
WHAT IS TOYA DOING, ANYWAY?!
TOYA?
Who?
YOUR FORMER SUPERIOR WHO HAS A COLLECTION OF YOUR PHOTOS AND IS KEEPING DIARIES ABOUT YOU. DOES THE NAME MAJOR TOYA INGRAM RING A BELL?
...DO YOU HAPPEN TO HATE HIM?
Such negative vibes.
Previously on Tsubasa, Toya tricked Kotobuki and almost caused her to get killed.
I HATE HIM WITH A PASSION!!
はっくしょん
Sneeze
(In Japan, it's said that when you sneeze, there's someone's talking about you somewhere.)
DID YOU CATCH A COLD, MAJOR INGRAM?
MAYBE RAIMON'S TALKING ABOUT ME.
ANY PROGRESS ON THE ORPHANAGE BOMBING CASE...?
IN OUR FAVOR, SIR.
GOOD.
GO AHEAD WITH THE ASSIGNMENT, LIEUTENANT MARSHEL.

YES, SIR.
THERE'S SO MANY...
...PROBLEMS WE HAVE TO DEAL WITH...
YOU THINK SO?
WELL, YEAH. LIKE YOURS.
I HOPE THE OFFICER FROM THIS AFTERNOON DIDN'T RECOGNIZE YOU.
WHAT IF HE DID?
Not many common officers know me.
WE RUN.
I'd rather not, but if it comes to it...
IF WE GO DUE NORTH, WE'LL COME ACROSS THE BORDER.
NOW THAT'S A PROBLEM.

THERE IS A BOMB INSIDE MY BODY SET TO GO OFF THE MOMENT I CROSS THE BORDER. YES, I AM A ROBOT.
FORGET IT.
ACTUALLY, THERE REALLY IS A PROBLEM.
Hanhini
We are currently here.
Duveni
Kneels
Countries of Earth in the 22nd century
THEY HAVE A COMPUTER SET UP AT THE BORDER TO KEEP TABS ON WHO GETS IN OR OUT. YOU NEED A PASS TO CROSS IT.
BEYOND THE BORDER IS A POOR COUNTRY CALLED HANHINI. ALTHOUGH DUVENI, ANOTHER NEIGHBORING COUNTRY, IS WEALTHY.
IT'S RUN BY A MILITARY REGIME. WE DON'T GET ALONG. THERE'S NO CHANCE THEY'LL LET US IN.
YOU DON'T KNOW WHAT COULD SPARK A WAR.
A WAR?!
DON'T WORRY. IT WON'T HAPPEN THAT EASILY.
......
RAIMON KNOWS EVERYTHING...

OF COURSE HE CAN READ. HE USED TO BE IN THE ARMY.
IT'S THE PLACE FOR THE PRIVILEGED FEW.
...RAIMON. DID YOU KNOW I WAS A NAMELESS ONE?
WHAT DO YOU THINK OF NAMELESS ONES?
WHETHER YOU'RE A NAMELESS ONE OR AN OFFICER... TITLES MEAN NOTHING TO ME.
I DON'T GIVE A DAMN IF PEOPLE ARE DYING IN THE STREETS OR WHATEVER.
HOWEVER...
...I'D NEVER WANT TO MAKE YOU SAD, KOTOBUKI.
....
HOW'S THAT FOR AN ANSWER?

I CAN'T HELP IT.
I'VE BUILT MY WORLD AROUND YOU, KOTOBUKI.
THANKS...
......
THAT'S SO YOU, RAIMON.

Phew.
YOU STOPPED RUNNING AWAY WHEN I KISS.
DOES THAT MEAN...
ポ
?
...IT'S TIME TO GO ALL THE WAY?
Aww...
Noooo!
NO WAY!!
Put me down!
DON'T WORRY. I'LL BE GENTLE.
I've been waiting for so long.
DON'T BE AFRAID.
There, there.
I'M NOT AN ANIMAL TO BE HANDLED!!

WHAT'S THAT?!
Damn
!
?!
EAT THIS!!
GET LOST, NAMELESS ONES!!
NEXT TIME, IT'LL BE MUCH BIGGER THAN A STONE!
HOW AWFUL...
......
......!!

STAY WHERE YOU ARE!!
I'LL SMASH YOUR SKULL IN!!
KOTOBUKI!...
WHY DOES EVERYBODY TREAT THE NAMELESS ONES LIKE TRASH?
WERE WE BROUGHT TO THE WORLD ONLY TO BE DESPISED?
ARE WE BORN WORTHLESS?
I'VE BEEN THINKING...

ARE NAMELESS ONES REALLY WORTHLESS?
WE LOST THEM.
Dammit!
I'M GOING TO REPORT THIS TO THE FORCES!!
DON'T WASTE YOUR TIME. YOU WON'T GET THEIR ATTENTION.
BUT...IF WE LET THEM GO, THEY'LL COME BACK AND DESTROY THE ORPHANAGE...
WAIT!! THERE'S ROSS!!
HE'S THE SPONSOR AND HE'S NOT FROM THE ARMY, RIGHT?
MAYBE HE CAN HELP US. LET ME AT HIM!
Wait, wait.
KOTOBUKI--

IT'S HUGE...
IS THIS REALLY HIS HOUSE?
BOLTING OUT WITHOUT AN ADDRESS WAS STUPID...
...but this is the largest house around.
Beep
Beep

DONG
?!
IT'S OPENING...
GOOD EVENING.
Oh...
HELLO... UM..
YOU'RE HERE FOR ROSS?

Ah!
YES! I AM!
I'LL TAKE YOU.
COME THIS WAY.
......?
IS HE A SERVANT...? OR MAYBE A SON?
What weird clothes...
......!
W-- WOW...
ALL THE LIGHTS ARE ON... IT LOOKS EXPENSIVE...

OF ALL THE HOUSES I BROKE INTO, THERE WAS NOTHING LIKE THIS...
WE'RE HERE.
OH.
THANKS...
I'VE KNOWN YOU...
...FOR A LONG TIME.
I KNOW YOU...
KOTOBUKI.

I'M SO GLAD...
...WE GOT TO MEET AGAIN...
...VANISHED INTO THIN AIR!!
Eeeeek!!
HE...
WHAT'S GOING ON? WHAT IS HE?!
WHO WAS THAT?!
OH...

I-I'VE COME TO SEE ROSS.
WHAT? HOW DID YOU GET IN?!
WHAT'S GOING ON?
ROSS?
THAT WOULD BE ME.
was sleeping
ARE YOU REALLY ROSS?
Yawn...
THAT'S RIGHT. WELL, WELL. I'M FLATTERED...
...THAT SUCH A LOVELY YOUNG LADY CAME ALL THE WAY HERE JUST TO SEE ME.
Let's go to bed!
YOU'RE WRONG!!

I WORK IN THE ORPHANAGE YOU SPONSOR.
OH, REALLY?
And?
SOMEONE ATTACKED THE PLACE, AND I--
STOP.
YES, I'VE BEEN THROWING IN AN ARM AND A LEG. BUT THAT'S ALL THERE IS TO IT. I CAN'T HELP YOU.
I CAN'T STAND NAMELESS ONES.
THEN... WHY...
IF YOU TRULY INSIST, I'LL LISTEN TO WHAT YOU HAVE TO SAY...
...IN BED. ♪
YOU OLD GOAT...

!!
OWW...
RAIMON...
How did you get in?
I KNEW IT WAS YOU.
IS THIS HOW YOU TREAT ME AFTER ALL THOSE YEARS?
YOU'RE AS STUPID AS EVER, ROSS.
?!
Master Raimon?
Master Raimon?
DO YOU KNOW EACH OTHER, RAIMON?
Wow!
YOU'RE HIS GIRLFRIEND!

LET ME INTRODUCE MYSELF, MY DEAR. I AM...
...RAIMON'S DAD! ♡
D--
IT'S NICE TO MEET YOU. ♡
DAAAD?!
Make us tea.
I will if you call me dad. ♪

翼を持つ者
つばさ
も
もの

YEAH... RAIMON'S A HUMAN AFTER ALL.
OF COURSE HE HAS PARENTS...
...BUT ACTUALLY SEEING THEM IS SOMETHING ELSE.
にっこり
I STILL CAN'T BELIEVE HE HAS A DAD!!
OKAY...
Well, well.
MAKE YOURSELF AT HOME, KOTOBUKI. MORE TEA?
Here.
He changed clothes.

AND A WEALTHY AND PRETTY (?) DAD, AT THAT.
RAIMON REALLY IS A PRODUCT OF THE UPPER-CLASS BACKGROUND...
WHERE'S MOTHER?
!...
Heh...
LIFE IN THE COUNTRY DOESN'T SEEM TO AGREE WITH HER. SHE'S BACK HOME.
MOTHER?!
I WANT TO SEE RAIMON'S MOM!!
?
ANYWAY, IT'S BEEN A WHILE, HASN'T IT?
YOU DIDN'T TELL ME ABOUT LEAVING THE ARMY. YOU JUST UP AND WALKED AWAY WITHOUT A WORD.
I SUPPOSE KOTOBUKI WAS THE DRIVING FORCE BEHIND THAT.
Ooh...
YOU'RE LOVELY. AND THAT SKIN... IT LOOKS SO SOFT! ♡
JUST LET HER TALK, WILL YOU?

HE'S LAID-BACK, TOO, BUT NOT QUITE LIKE RAIMON...
I WORK AT THE ORPHANAGE THAT YOU SPONSOR... RAIMON DOES, TOO.
SOME PEOPLE ARE GIVING US A HARD TIME.
THERE'S BEEN A SERIES OF ATTACKS TARGETING ORPHANAGES, AND WE'RE ALL WORRIED.
I WAS HOPING MAYBE YOU COULD HELP US P--
I HATE TO REPEAT MYSELF, BUT...
I CAN'T STAND NAMELESS ONES.
I DON'T WANT ANY PART OF IT.
....
THEN WHY ARE YOU HELPING THEM?
I HAD NO CHOICE. IT WAS SOMETHING MY GRANDFATHER DID.
WHY...?

WHY DO YOU HATE NAMELESS ONES SO MUCH...?!
WHAT DID WE DO TO MAKE EVERYONE HATE US?
SO IS THAT IT?
WE'RE BORN SIMPLY TO BE DESPISED?
THEY HAVE NO EDUCATION OR MANNERS.
THEY'RE DISGUSTING.
THEY'RE ALSO THE FIRST ONES TO COMMIT A CRIME.
BUT I GUESS YOU KNOW THAT VERY WELL.
THE NAMELESS THIEF KOTOBUKI.

DID YOU HEAR THAT? SERIOUSLY?
HOW COME RAIMON LIKES HER?
Heh...
TALK ABOUT BAD TASTE.
クス
Shh. They can hear us.
クス
I'M LEAVING...
I HOPE YOU STAY LONGER NEXT TIME.
I'M NOT PICKY WHEN IT COMES TO A BED PARTNER. ♡
IN YOUR DREAMS!!
IMAGINE HOW SURPRISED I WAS WHEN TOYA TOLD ME ABOUT HER.
LOOK...
DID YOU KNOW THAT IT'S OFTEN THE EDUCATED PEOPLE...
...WHO HAVE NO BRAINS OR CLASS?

MY ADVICE TO THEM WOULD BE...
...TO START WORRYING BEFORE SOMEONE STABS THEM IN THE BACK.
IS THAT...
... A WARNING?
Not really.
WHO SAID I WAS TALKING ABOUT YOU?
ARE YOU WORRIED ABOUT SOMETHING?
ぱたん
...YOU DAMNED BRAT.
Ha ha ha...
OH DEAR. PARDON MY FRENCH.
IT JUST CAME OUT.
GET ME A PHONE, WILL YOU?

"DISGUSTING."
THAT HASN'T BEEN THE FIRST TIME SOMEONE INSULTED US...
...BUT THE FACT THAT IT WAS RAIMON'S DAD MAKES ALL THE DIFFERENCE...
I HAVE TO...
...CALL MAJOR INGRAM.
OF COURSE, NO FATHER WOULD WANT...
...HIS SON TO BE WITH A NAMELESS THIEF...
KOTOBUKI.
YOU'RE GOING THE WRONG WAY.
HM? OH!!
Oh?
I GUESS I GOT LOST.
It's so big.
?
HOW DID YOU FIND YOUR WAY TO HIS ROOM?

THERE WAS THIS STRANGE BOY WHO LET ME IN...
HOW...?
"I'M SO GLAD WE GOT TO MEET AGAIN."
?
Oh yeah!!
HE JUST VANISHED!
I DON'T REALLY KNOW...
WAS HE A GHOST, OR WAS IT A DREAM?
"I KNOW YOU."
"I'VE KNOWN YOU FOR A LONG TIME..."
"...KOTOBUKI."
HE DIDN'T LOOK FAMILIAR, BUT IT'S POSSIBLE I'VE FORGOTTEN...

Anyway...
KOTOBUKI.
I'M SORRY ABOUT WHAT HAPPENED BACK THERE.
EH?!
IT'S FINE. I'M MORE WORRIED ABOUT YOU. IS EVERYTHING OKAY BETWEEN YOU TWO?
OH, THAT. I DON'T CARE.
WE'VE NEVER GOTTEN ALONG. EVER.
DON'T LET HIS WORDS GET TO YOU.
WHOA!!
YOU'RE DOING GREAT.
YOU'VE BEEN DOING GREAT.

HIS WORDS...
...MAKE ME FEEL SO MUCH BETTER.
DON'T WORRY. I'LL BE FINE.
IT'S JUST...
ANYWAY!
SINCE I CAN'T TURN TO YOUR DAD, I'M GOING TO TAKE THE MATTER INTO MY HANDS!
HIS UNRELIABILITY HAS NEVER BEEN IN DOUBT.
LET'S GO HOME.
...IT'S JUST THAT...
DOES MY PRESENCE EVER EMBARRASS HIM?
THAT THOUGHT...

...BREAKS MY HEART.
AS FOR...
...THE ORPHANAGE... LIEUTENANT PHERE MARSHEL...
I'M SENDING YOU THERE.
THERE WAS A CALL FROM ROSS.
RAIMON SHOWED UP AT HIS DOOR.
HE SAID HE'S WORKING AT THE ORPHANAGE.

RAIMON'S... WORKING?
Heh...
YOU'RE SURPRISED, TOO, PHERE?
I WOULD NORMALLY SEND INGRAM FOR A CHECKUP...
BUT HE'S TOO SWEET ON RAIMON.
SORRY ABOUT THAT.
WE DON'T WANT RAIMON STICKING HIS NOSE WHERE IT DOESN'T BELONG RIGHT NOW.
PHERE, YOU'RE IN CHARGE OF THE ORPHANAGE CASE, SO GO AND KEEP TABS ON HIM.
COPY THAT.
DON'T HURT HIM.

HE'S...
RAIMON IS...
...GOING TO BE MY RIGHT-HAND MAN.
I'LL...
...GET ON IT RIGHT AWAY...
...COLONEL.
ALL RIGHT.
THAT WAS THE LAST OF THE WASHING.
パチ
パチ
パチ
パチ

Oooh...
IT FEELS GOOD TO WAKE UP EARLY AND HANG THE WASHING.
ESPECIALLY WHEN YOU'RE BUMMED OUT.
YOU'RE BUMMED OUT?
HM?
I-IT'S JUST A FIGURE OF SPEECH, YOU KNOW!!
KOTOBUKI?!
IT'S KOTOBUKI!
WERE YOU ALL RIGHT YESTER-DAY?
WE WERE WORRIED ABOUT YOU.
NO PROBLEM. DID YOU SLEEP WELL?
KOTOBUKI!
Hey.
DID YOU WASH YOUR FACE?
WE'VE BEEN TALKING...
ABOUT...?
WHAT COULD HAPPEN IF WE FOUND TSUBASA.

IF WE FOUND TSUBASA...
...WE'D ASK FOR OUR MOMS AND DADS.
SOME PEOPLE BELIEVE IT'S STILL SOMEWHERE IN THE GROUND...
...AND THAT WHOEVER FINDS IT WILL HAVE HIS WISH GRANTED. IT'S A MYTH OF OUR TIME...
TSUBASA...
I WANT TO PROTECT THIS ORPHANAGE.
IT'S SAID THAT A LONG TIME AGO...
...TSUBASA SHOWED UP AND GRANTED EVERYONE'S WISHES BEFORE VANISHING.
AND THIS TIME...
...I'M NOT GOING TO JUST STAND THERE.
GOT ANY PLANS?
I'LL BE ON GUARD!
THAT'S NOT A PLAN, KOTOBUKI.
But!!
YOU NEVER KNOW WHEN THEY'LL COME AT US.
It's better than just sitting around.

I REMEMBER THE FACE OF THE GUY WHO BROKE THE GLASS.
I'LL GET HIM AND MAKE HIM PAY FOR THE GLASS.
WOW. YOU COULD SEE HIM?
OF COURSE. I HAD TO TRAIN MY EYES WHEN I WAS A THIEF.
Oh!
"THEY'RE ALSO THE FIRST ONES TO COMMIT CRIMES."
I'LL STAY WITH YOU, KOTOBUKI.
JUST DON'T DO ANYTHING ALONE, OKAY?
...SURE.
......
I WONDER WHAT HE'S...
...UP TO NOW?

ANYWAY...
...WHAT'S WRONG WITH THOSE BASHERS?
Dammit!
I WISH I COULD GET MY HANDS ON THEM..
I HOPE RAIMON'S KEEPING WATCH.
IF THEY WANT TO ATTACK THE ARMY, THEN JUST DO SO.
?
!!
HE'S AT IT AGAIN...
WHERE'S HE GOING?
THAT'S THE BASTARD WHO BROKE THE GLASS!!
"JUST DON'T DO ANYTHING ALONE, OKAY?"
BUT...
THIS COULD BE MY ONLY CHANCE!!

......
A HOUSE WITH ELECTRICITY, HUH?
HMM... WHAT SHOULD I DO...?
SO HOW WAS IT?
HE'S GOT FRIENDS.
Yikes!
ALL CLEAR. THEY'RE PRACTICALLY WAITING TO BE ATTACKED.
LET'S FINISH THIS ONE OFF AND MOVE ON.
HOW MANY HAVE WE GOT?
THIS ONE IS OUR FOURTH. SO...SEVEN MORE TO GO.
THAT MANY PIG HOUSES?!
NOW THAT'S WORK.
THOSE BASTARDS ...!!

WHO ARE YOU?
ANSWER ME!!
THAT BITCH... IS WORKING IN THAT DUMP.
......
SO YOU'RE THE ORPHANAGE BASHERS?!
THAT'S RIGHT.
THEY'RE OUR WORK.
WHAT ARE YOU GOING TO DO ABOUT IT?
I WON'T LET YOU DESTROY IT.
IF YOU HAVE ISSUES WITH THE ARMY, GO TO THEM!!

SHUT UP!!
!!
WE DON'T NORMALLY ROUGH UP GIRLS...
...BUT YOU'VE SEEN TOO MUCH.
THE GUN I SAW IN TOWN...
......
AS A SEND-OFF GIFT, I'LL LET YOU IN ON THE TRUTH.
OUR GOAL ISN'T THE ARMY.
WE'RE BEING PAID TO DO THIS.

WE'RE CLEANING OUT THE ORPHANAGES AS PART OF SOME "BIG PLAN."
WHO ARE WE TO SAY NO TO A LITTLE CLEAN UP IF WE GET PAID FOR IT?
A PLAN?
AND THAT SUDDENLY MAKES IT OKAY?
WHO CARES? IT'S JUST ANOTHER DUMP, GONE.
WE'RE DOING THOSE NAMELESS KIDS A BIG FAVOR.
THINK ABOUT IT. THEY HAVE NO FUTURE. THEY'LL NEVER FIND A JOB, LET ALONE MARRY.
WHAT KIND OF MAN WOULD WANT A NAMELESS ONE FOR A LOVER?
HE'D BE RIDICULED..
...AND DISOWNED.
WHO WOULD WANT TO BE WITH A NAMELESS ONE?
A LOSER WHO DESERVES TO BE LAUGHED AT.

SO WHAT'S THE PLAN?
SHE'LL BE SILENCED...
Heh...
...ONCE WE'VE HAD SOME FUN.
Oh.
GOOD IDEA.
WHA--
W-WAIT...
DESPIC-ABLE!
GET OFF...!
RAIMON...!
RAIMON...

PHERE...
......
WAY TO GREET A FORMER COLLEAGUE.
ピシッ
WE'VE NOT SEEN EACH OTHER SINCE YOU LEFT THE ARMY...
THE WHIP WAS A DEAD GIVE-AWAY, PHERE.
...YET YOU RECOGNIZED ME INSTANTLY. GOOD FOR YOU.
I KNEW ROSS WOULD CONTACT YOU.
WHAT BUSINESS BROUGHT THE LIEUTENANT, NOT THE MAJOR, DOWN HERE?
ALL THE MORE REASON TO BELIEVE SOMETHING IS GOING ON.

THE ATTACKS?
OR THAT THING BEHIND ME?
I HAVE COME HERE BY ORDERS OF THE COLONEL.
I AM NOT HERE TO FIGHT.
FOR NOW.
YOU'VE STILL GOT...
...UNRESOLVED ISSUES WITH ME.

AGAIN...
DON'T WORRY.
THESE BAD GUYS CAN'T DO ANYTHING TO YOU.
IT'S HIM AGAIN!!
HOW DID HE GET IN?!
Th--
THANKS... UM...
WHO ARE YOU?
I KNOW YOU, KOTOBUKI.
YOU'RE THE PERSON WHO KEEPS THE PLANET GOING ROUND.
...?
THAT MAKES NO SENSE...
YOUR BOYFRIEND, RAIMON. DOES HE TREAT YOU WELL?
DO YOU LIKE HIM? IS HE SPECIAL TO YOU?
....

STOP ASKING...
...THE OBVIOUS.
THEN...
...YOU ARE HAPPY.
...I AM.
BUT I'M NOT SURE ABOUT RAIMON.
MAYBE I'M MAKING HIS LIFE MISERABLE AND I DON'T KNOW IT...
WHY WOULD HE WANT A NAMELESS ONE FOR A LOVER?
"WHAT KIND OF MAN WOULD WANT A NAMELESS ONE AS A LOVER?"

ALL I WANT IS TO BECOME GOOD ENOUGH FOR RAIMON...
...BUT IF HE'S GOING TO BE RIDICULED BECAUSE OF ME...
MY...
...HEART WOULD BREAK.
WHY AM I OPENING UP TO A COMPLETE STRANGER?
YOU SHOULD BE MORE SELFISH...
I KNOW YOU'VE BEEN TRYING SO HARD...
...SINCE YOU WERE IN THAT ORPHANAGE.
SINCE THAT VERY COLD DAY...
...WHEN ANN LEEN TOOK YOU IN AS A BABY.

YOU'VE BEEN WORKING HARD EVER SINCE, HAVEN'T YOU?
......
HOW...
...DO YOU KNOW ABOUT THAT?
ABOUT A PLACE SO SWEET AND SO WARM...
...AND SO SAD...

翼を持つ者

I DON'T WANT RAIMON RIDICULED BECAUSE OF ME...
THAT WOULD BE TOO PAINFUL.
BUT...
HOW?
HOW DID YOU KNOW...?
ABOUT THE ORPHAN-AGE?
WHO IS HE?
YOU WERE VERY POOR WHEN YOU WERE IN THE ORPHANAGE...
...BUT YOU WERE...
...VERY HAPPY THERE.

...YEAH.
Ah ha ha ha...
WE'RE HOME!
WE FOUND LOTS OF FIREWOOD.
ENOUGH TO KEEP US WARM THROUGHOUT THE WINTER!!
GOOD JOB, KOTOBUKI, TOTA!!

ANN TOOK ME IN AS A BABY.
SHE RAN A SMALL ORPHANAGE WITH FIVE OTHER NAMELESS KIDS.
THE ARMY GAVE US SOME MONEY...
...BUT NOT NEARLY ENOUGH TO LIVE ON.
WE REALLY STRUGGLED.
A BUD!!
WOW!!
WE'VE GOT BUDS!!
Good!
LET'S GIVE IT A YELL!
Hang in there!
I HAD EVERYONE I NEEDED.

I HAD...
...ANN.
...PARADING INTO THE TOWN.
Look.
THERE THEY GO AGAIN...
THEY'D BETTER STAY CLEAR.
I'LL THROW STONES AT THEM IF THEY COME NEAR.
THAT LADY HAS A FAMILY NAME AND WAS FROM A DECENT BACKGROUND.
I DON'T KNOW WHY SHE BOTHERS.
SHE'S A HYPOCRITE. I DON'T WANT THEM NEAR US.
STOP INSULTING ANN...!!
KOTOBUKI, TOTA...
STRAIGHTEN UP.

THEY MAY CALL US NAMELESS ONES...
...BUT...
...WE ARE STILL HUMANS.
WHY SHOULD YOU FEEL ASHAMED OF BEING HUMAN?
I WANT YOU TO KEEP YOUR HEADS HELD HIGH!
LET'S DO IT.
LET'S FIND THE MEANING OF LIFE.
THE PROOF OF LIFE!
"PROOF OF LIFE." THOSE WERE HER FAVORITE WORDS.
SHE WAS SO STRONG AND PROUD.

SWEET ANN...
YOU HAD THIS GOLD WATCH WHEN I FOUND YOU.
GOLD?
IT'S A VERY VALUABLE THING, KOTOBUKI.
YOUR PARENTS DIDN'T WANT TO GIVE YOU UP.
WHY?
WELL, FOR ONE THING, THEY WOULDN'T LEAVE SUCH A VALUABLE THING WITH YOU IF THEY DIDN'T CARE.
AND THEY COULD'VE LEFT YOU ON THE STREET, NOT IN FRONT OF OUR BUILDING.
......
I DIDN'T HOLD A GRUDGE...
...BUT IT WAS HARD...

...KNOWING THAT I HAD BEEN A BURDEN TO THEM.
HOW-EVER...
THEY DIDN'T HATE ME...
SINCE YOU ARE SIX, I WANT YOU TO KEEP IT.
TREAT IT WELL.
IT'S YOUR MOM AND DAD'S PROOF OF LOVE!
PEOPLE IN TOWN WOULD LOOK AT US COLDLY...
...AND SAY WE WEREN'T WANTED.
BUT THE WATCH GAVE ME COURAGE.
IT'S FREEZING!!

HUDDLE UP!!
Yaaay!
MORE THAN ANYTHING, I HAD EVERYONE.
IT WAS WARM...
...AND SWEET.
I HAD ANN.
WE'LL CURL UP TOGETHER. COME ON, KIDS!!
MY FAMILY...
TOTA?!
WHAT HAPPENED TO YOU?!

NOTHING.
THEY MUST'VE BEATEN HIM UP.
......
It's all right.
IT WASN'T A RARE OCCURRENCE, BUT WE DIDN'T TELL ANN.
WE DIDN'T WANT TO MAKE HER SAD.
Dammit!!
STUPID GROWN-UPS, BEATING UP KIDS!!
YOU KNOW WHAT ANN ALWAYS TELLS US.
DON'T HOLD A GRUDGE. RISE ABOVE THEM.
YOU'RE RIGHT...
I'LL BE SOMEONE BIG...
...AND I'LL HELP MAKE LIFE EASIER FOR THE NAMELESS ONES.

THEN WILL YOU MARRY ME, KOTOBUKI?!
MARRY? WHAT'S THAT?
I'LL HELP THE NAMELESS ONES LIVE HAPPY LIVES.
AND WE'LL BE EVEN HAPPIER.
THAT'S MY PROOF OF LIFE...!
IT'S A PROMISE TO STAY TOGETHER FOREVER.
ANN AND EVERYONE CAN GET MARRIED, AND THEN WE'LL ALL HAVE A NAME.
......
WOW...
WOW, TOTA...! I'LL WORK HARD AND BECOME BIG, TOO!
THEN I CAN PROTECT SOMEONE I LIKE!

I DIDN'T WANT TO BE LEFT BEHIND ANYMORE.
I WON'T LET SOMEONE I CARE ABOUT BE RIDICULED!
LET'S FIND OUR PROOF OF LIFE.
LET'S DO IT.
BUT A FEW WEEKS LATER...
...ANN COLLAPSED.
Huff
Huff
...I'M FINE.
I JUST NEED TO REST.

ANN...
WHERE'RE YOU GOING, TOTA?
I'M GOING TO GET A DOCTOR. STAY WITH HER UNTIL I--
I'LL GO!!
I'M THE FASTEST ONE. I'LL BE BACK IN A BIT!
KOTOBUKI.
I HAVE TO TRY!!
I HAVE-TO DO IT NOW.
I HAVE TO PROTECT SOMEONE I LOVE!!
ANN IS ILL?
SHE MUST'VE GOTTEN SOMETHING FROM YOU NAMELESS ONES.
SHE'S SUFFERING. SHE'S IN LOTS OF PAIN.
PLEASE COME AND SEE HER!!

IT MUST BE THE EPIDEMIC COLD...
I DON'T HAVE ANYTHING FOR YOU NAMELESS ONES.
ANN'S NOT NAMELESS!!
SO WHAT? YOU HAVE NO MONEY!!
MONEY...
ドキッ
"YOUR PARENTS' PROOF OF LIFE"
BUT ...!!
LOOK, THIS IS "GOLD" AND IT'S "VALUABLE." I'LL GIVE THIS TO YOU.
SO GIVE ME MEDICINE!!
PLEASE...!!
ANN'S MY FAMILY...!!

HERE.
ポイ
....
Huff
HANG IN THERE, ANN!!
Huff
I'M COMING SOON!!
Huff
......!
THANK YOU...!!
Huff
WHAT'S THAT SMELL?
Huff
......?
WHAT'S THAT?
Huff
Huff
Huff
IT'S BRIGHT... IS IT DAWN ALREADY?
Huff
パ
ラ

Huff
"WHY SHOULD YOU FEEL ASHAMED OF BEING HUMAN?"
Huff
Huff
"LET'S DO IT."
Huff
"LET'S FIND THE MEANING OF LIFE."

"PROOF OF LIFE."
IT BURNED TO THE GROUND.
THE ARSONIST'S STILL AT LARGE, RIGHT?
THEY'RE TARGETING NAMELESS ONES.
THAT KID IS THE ONLY SURVIVOR. THE REST OF THEM ARE DEAD.
WHOEVER DID THIS DIDN'T FINISH THE JOB.
SHE'S UNWANTED HERE.

SHE'LL START BLAMING US.
THEY HATED US SO MUCH...
...THEY WERE CAPABLE OF SUCH AN ATROCITY.
I WAS FALLING INTO PIECES.
SOMETHING LIKE THAT COULD HAPPEN AGAIN...
I CAN'T PUT RAIMON THROUGH...
...THE SNEERS AND RIDICULE...
...THAT ANN HAD TO PUT UP WITH.
I'M FALLING APART.
YOU REALLY CARE ABOUT RAIMON.

AFTER THE FIRE...
...I WAS LEFT ALL ALONE...
...SO I LEFT ON A JOURNEY.
NO MONEY, NO JOB, NO NOTHING.
I SOON FOUND MYSELF STEALING.

I KNEW IT WAS WRONG...
...BUT I HAD TO SURVIVE.
ALL I COULD THINK OF WAS HOW TO GET THROUGH EACH DAY.
AND...
"NICE TO MEET YOU. ARE YOU KOTOBUKI?"
KOTOBUKI.
"YOU'RE CUTE."
I SAW THE HOUSE GLOWING IN THE DISTANCE.
WHAT ARE YOU DOING HERE?

WHAT'S WRONG?
I FINALLY FOUND...
...MY PROOF OF LIFE.
IT'S RAIMON.
...I...
...WILL... WORK HARD...

I'LL BE GOOD ENOUGH FOR HIM.
I WON'T LET THEM TAKE HIM AWAY
I WILL PROTECT SOMEONE I CARE ABOUT.
DON'T LEAVE MY SIDE...
I WON'T.
I'VE BUILT MY WORLD AROUND YOU, KOTOBUKI.
I'M GOING TO MARRY YOU ONE DAY, KOTOBUKI.
ポン
"IT'S A PROMISE TO STAY TOGETHER FOREVER."

"AND THEN WE'LL BE..."
"...EVEN HAPPIER."
UH-HUH...
ANYWAY...
WHY THE SUDDEN DOUBT?
MAYBE I NEED TO DEMONSTRATE MY LOVE MORE.
HUH?
WHAT?!
NOT NOW, NOT HERE, YOU IDIOT!!
BUT I WANT TO COMFORT YOU. ♡
Nn...
THAT'S NOT NECESSARY!! GET OFF!

ugh...
Oh?
WE'RE NOT ALONE.
DIDN'T YOU NOTICE...?
I ALMOST FORGOT!!
THEY'RE THE ORPHANAGE BASHERS!
REALLY?
AND THEY SAID SOMEONE'S PAYING THEM TO DO IT!!
I SEE.
I SAW THE BOY AGAIN.
AND...
Hey
ARE YOU LISTENING TO ME?!
YEAH. SOMEONE PUT THEM UP TO IT, RIGHT?
WHO ARE YOU?
HOW DID YOU...

......
BANG
RAI--
A BULLET-PROOF JACKET...
Phew...
YOU INTER-RUPTED US.
ANSWER MY QUESTION. YES OR NO.
IT WAS ROSS...
...WHO HIRED YOU, RIGHT?

......YES
WHAT?
GOOD ANSWER.
LET'S GO.
Huh?!
B-BUT...
THIS GENTLEMAN NEEDS TO SEE A DOCTOR. HIS RIBS MAY BE PUNCTURING A LUNG.
Okay.
RIGHT?
AND ROSS IS THE MASTERMIND OF THE ATTACKS?!
WHY ARE YOU FROZEN?
KA-CHAK
Damn..!!
THAT SON OF A BITCH SHOT THE SAME PLACE FIVE TIMES!!
ROSS IS RAIMON'S DAD, RIGHT?

DO YOU REALLY BELIEVE HIM? ABOUT YOUR FATHER BEING...
IT'S HIGHLY LIKELY.
ROSS'S COM-PANY MANU-FACTURES THIS GUN.
LOW COST AND CHEAP PRICE. IT GOES AROUND AND IS ILLEGAL.
Criminals.
THEY ALL HAD THE SAME GUN.
BUT THAT DOESN'T MEAN ROSS IS INVOLVED...
Maybe his subordinates?
IT'S HIM.
I INVENTED THIS CONVERTED GUN.
WHAT DID YOU MAKE IT FOR?!
And why?!
FOR FUN. ROSS STOLE IT FROM ME...
...a long time ago.
I'LL NEVER UNDERSTAND WHAT GOES THROUGH A GENIUS'S MIND!!
HE'S A CRUEL BASTARD.
YOU'RE GOING TO DO HIM IN, RIGHT?

WHAT HE DID TO THE ORPHANAGES WAS HORRIBLE.
NO ONE SHOULD HAVE TO GO THROUGH SUCH MISERY...
...OR SUCH SADNESS.
BUT...
IT'S HIS DAD.
HIS OWN FLESH AND BLOOD.
IS HE REALLY CAPABLE OF...
...TURNING HIS BACK ON HIM?

OH, DEAR.
That means...
...THAT RAIMON AND KOTOBUKI FOUND OUT. THAT'S PROBLE-MATIC.
OKAY, GO TO HOSPITAL AND DON'T COME BACK FOR A WHILE.
klik☆
IT LOOKS LIKE...
...WE'RE IN FOR A LITTLE BATTLE, LIEUTENANT MARSHEL.
ARE YOU UP FOR IT? THIS COULD BE A CHANCE FOR YOU TO BRING RAIMON DOWN.
I CAN'T WAIT.

ARE YOU READY, KOTOBUKI?
DO I REALLY HAVE TO DO THIS?
SHUT UP. STOP WHINING AND JUST DO IT.
YOU SHUT UP, OLD WOMAN.
Eh?!
I CAN HEAR YOU, YOU LITTLE BRAT!!
I MEANT FOR YOU TO.
STOP IT.
GET ON WITH IT. WE DON'T HAVE ALL DAY.
HERE, HOLD THIS.
WHAT'S THIS?
IT'S A MAKESHIFT MIKE.
ぱちん
YOU DIDN'T EVEN BRING A MIKE...?
Useless woman.
IT'S NOT MY FAULT!
KOTOBUKI ...
IT'S ROLLING.
WHAT?!!!
YOU WERE SUPPOSED TO GIVE ME A HEADS-UP!!
ERM... UM!!

Hi... Long time no see.
HOW'S IT GOING, GUYS? I'M DOING OKAY.
AND I LOOK A LITTLE DIFFERENT, DON'T I?!
THANKS FOR PICKING UP *TSUBASA: THOSE WITH WINGS*!!
EASY, KOTOBUKI. NO RUSH.
YEAH, BUT IT'S BEEN EIGHT YEARS AND I'M A BIT NERVOUS.
I HAVEN'T CHANGED INSIDE.
IT'S JUST THE ART-WORK...
UH... I'M NOT MAKING MUCH SENSE.
DON'T WORRY. YOU LOOK PRETTY.
THAT'S IRRELEVANT.
YOU'RE GOING TO BREAK THE "MIKE"!!
HEY!! YOU'RE TOO CLOSE!!!
IT'S FINE. YOU'RE SO PRETTY.

GAAAAH... STUPID LOVEBIRDS!
WHOA ...
YOU THINK THIS IS A BIG JOKE? THEY'LL THINK WE'VE GOT NO CLASS BECAUSE OF YOU TWO!!
BUT IT'S TRUE...
Naturally...
AND YOU, RAIMON...
YOU'RE CUTTING ME OFF!!
FORGET IT!! I'LL TAKE CARE OF THE REST!!
IT WAS STUPID TO HAVE YOU DO THIS JUST BECAUSE YOU'RE THE MAIN CHARACTER!!
YOU WANT TO DO IT, RIGHT?
RAIMON, GIVE ME THE CAMERA!! STOP TAPING ONLY KOTOBUKI.

You--
YOU KICKED HER!!
BOSS... WE SHOULD RUN.
STOP IT, RAIMON!!
BOSS, RUN... WATCH OUT, IT'S A CLIFF!!
DON'T WORRY, THIS IS NOTHING STRANGE.
I HOPE YOU WON'T GIVE UP ON US. SEE YOU IN THE SECOND VOLUME!
...AHHHH!!!

Thank you.

Nice to meet you and hello!
It's been a while since I've worked on
Tsubasa: Those With Wings. It feels a
bit awkward to look at my earlier work.
I still receive letters from Tsubasa fans.
Thanks so much for your support! I wrote
this series a long time ago and I know
it's not perfect. I hope you come away
with something good after you read this.

Natsuki Takaya

In Volume 2 of

Kotobuki has finally landed her dream job at the orphanage but nothing is ever that easy for her. Someone is trying to get the orphange closed down and Kotobuki will do whatever it takes to prevent it. But she faces a tough choice when it turns out that Raimon's father may be behind it all.

Coming in December 2008

Phantom Dream™

GENEIMUSOU by Natsuki Takaya

TAMAKI-CHAAN.
TAMAKI-CHAAAN!

TAA-MAAKII--
--CHAAN!
ASAHI.
TODAY I HAD TO WAKE UP AT FIVE AND WORK AGAIN, SO I'M SLEEPY.
DON'T IRRITATE ME ANYMORE THAN I ALREADY AM.
SHUT UP, YOU IDIOT GIRL!!
BONK
OH.
IT'S BECAUSE YOU KEPT ME WAITING FOR 20 WHOLE MINUTES, TAMAKI-CHAN.
DON'T COMPLAIN BECAUSE I MADE YOU WAIT FOR ME--BE GRATEFUL!!
How mean!
And do something about those huge eyes of yours!!
WHAAT KIND OF NONSENSE ARE YOU SPEWING THIS TIME, MY IDIOT OF A SON?
Oh
MOTHER...

REALLY, HOW AM I GOING TO EXPLAIN TO YOUR GRANDPA AND FATHER UP IN HEAVEN THAT YOU GREW UP SO VIOLENT?
CRINKLE
THEY'RE UP THERE CRYING BECAUSE THEIR WIFE/DAUGHTER-IN-LAW GOT SO CRASS.
TAMAKI-CHAN, WHO'S ALWAYS IN A WORSE MOOD THAN USUAL IN THE MORNING, IS THE SOLE HEIR TO THIS TEMPLE...
...AND HE'S ALSO THE HEAD PRIEST.
YOU ARE SO NOT CUTE. YOU'RE ABOUT TO LOSE YOUR DINNER, YOU KNOW.
FLAP
WHA--EEK!
YOU JUST DON'T WANT TO COOK!!
OH NO.
AND THEN...
IT SAYS THERE'S BEEN A BIZARRE INCIDENT AT TODA HIGH SCHOOL...
TODA HIGH...?
Where's that?
THE WEAPON HAS NOT BEEN LOCATED, AND THE VICTIM SUFFERED MULTIPLE INJURIES THAT SEEM LIKE GOUGES...
DOESN'T THAT SEEM STRIKING TO YOU, TAMAKI?
!
NOT REALLY.

HAS NOTHING TO DO WITH ME.
OH, WAIT. WAIT!
WE'RE GOING NOW, MOTHER!
OKAY. BE CAREFUL NOW.
WHEN IS THAT IDIOT SON OF MINE...
... GOING TO BECOME SELF-AWARE, I WONDER.
......
AND THEN ...
THE SOLE...
...HEIR.
REALLY, I'M SO SLEEPY.
THANK YOU FOR YOUR HARD WORK EVERY MORNING. ♡
......
SORRY I HIT YOU.
It feels like I say this all the time, but...

TAMAKI-CHAN IS IMPORTANT TO ME.
WHEN WE GET TO SCHOOL, COULD YOU PLEASE SHOW ME YOUR PHYSICS HOMEWORK? PLEASE?
DON'T YOU EVER FEEL LIKE DOING IT YOURSELF?
YEP, BUT I CAN'T DO IT.
It'd take the rest of my life, you know?
AT MY HOUSE, MY FATHER IS DEAD AND MY MOTHER WON'T STAY HOME WITH ME AT ALL, BUT...
...I'M FINE AS LONG AS TAMAKI-CHAN'S THERE FOR ME.
ASAHI...
OTOYA-KUN HIT YOU AGAIN, DIDN'T HE?
HOW'D YOU KNOW, JUN-CHAN?!!
What?!!
THERE'S A BANDAGE ON YOUR HEAD.
Doh.
HE'S SO SCARY.
I CAN'T BELIEVE YOU CAN ACT NORMAL AROUND HIM.
HE'S KIND...
...AND STRONG, YOU KNOW.
TAMAKI-CHAN.

ガラッ
YOU'RE SO FAR GONE, YOU'RE SICK, ASAHI.
HEY, HOMEROOM'S STARTING, YOU KNOW.
FIRST OFF, I'LL INTRODUCE THE TRANSFER STUDENT.
Wow.
HERE.
COME IN.
THIS IS MITSURU TORII.
SHE'S FROM TODA HIGH SCHOOL.
MITSURU-CHAN?!

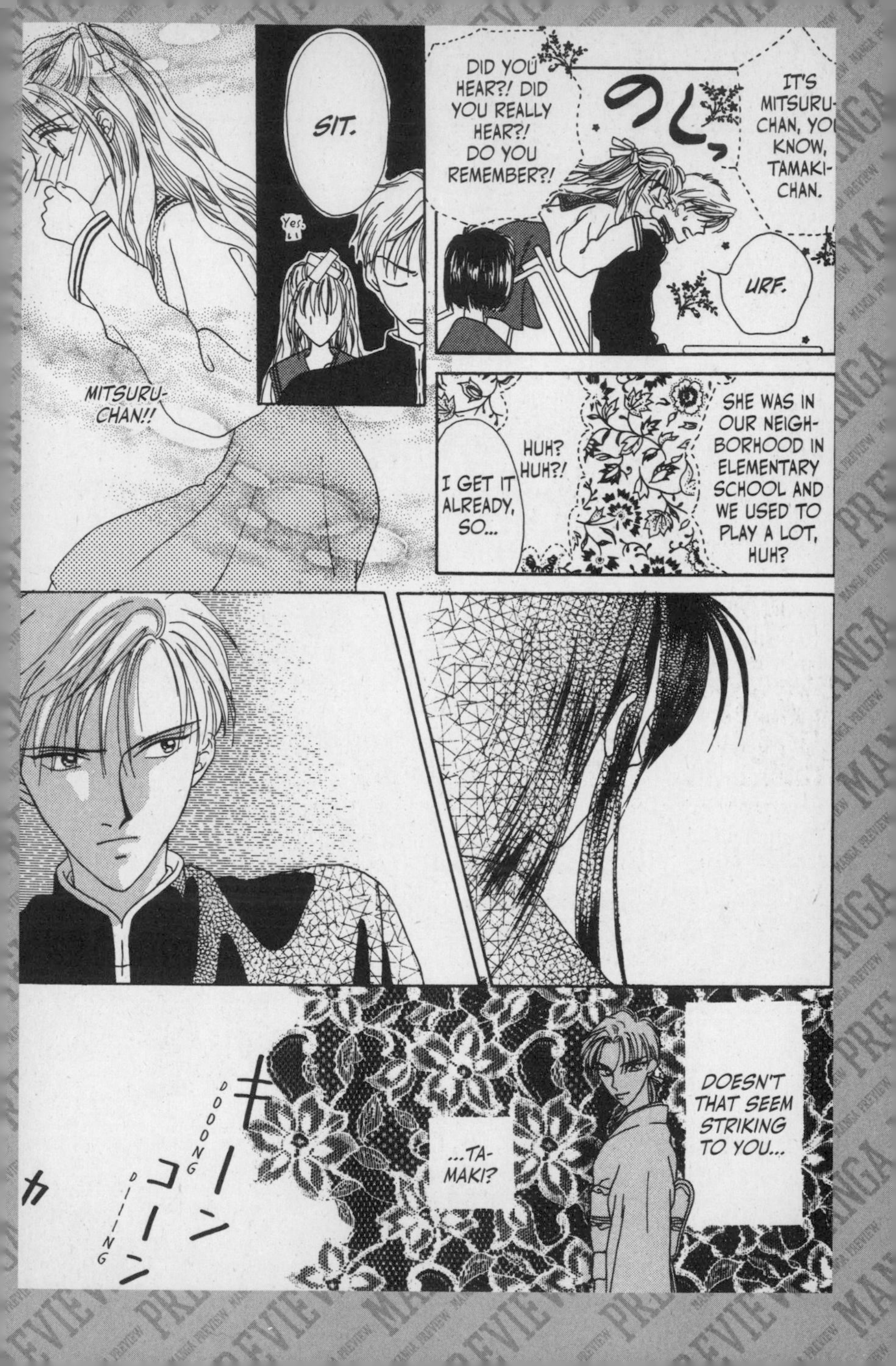

IT'S MITSURU-CHAN, YOU KNOW, TAMAKI-CHAN.
DID YOU HEAR?! DID YOU REALLY HEAR?! DO YOU REMEMBER?!
URF.
SIT.
Yes.
SHE WAS IN OUR NEIGHBORHOOD IN ELEMENTARY SCHOOL AND WE USED TO PLAY A LOT, HUH?
HUH? HUH?!
I GET IT ALREADY, SO...
MITSURU-CHAN!!
DOESN'T THAT SEEM STRIKING TO YOU...
...TAMAKI?
DDDDONG
DIIING

TORII-SAAAN.
MITSU...
HEY, HEY. YOUR HAIR'S LONG, ISN'T IT? IT'S SO PRETTY.
WHA...? UMM...
TORII-SAN?
OH...
!?
ASAHI!
!
ASAHI!
MITSURU-CHAN!!

gasp
THEY'RE FAST, FAST!--THAT IS, YOUR LEGS ARE, MITSURU-CHAN!!
gasp
I TOOK THE STAIRS TWO AT A TIME AND THOUGHT I'D TRIP!
UMM...?
IT'S ME, ASAHI!
WHEN WE WERE IN ELEMENTARY SCHOOL WE PLAYED TOGETHER A LOT WITH TAMAKI-CHAN, REMEMBER?
YOU'RE *HINA*, AREN'T YOU?!!
wow!
MITSURU-CHAN, THAT'S THE NICKNAME YOU GAVE ME!
...!
I WANTED TO SEE YOU SO BAD!
YOU'RE SO TALL NOW!
giggle
MITSURU-CHAN, MITSURU-CHAAN.
YOU'RE STILL THE SAME HINA, AREN'T YOU...

gasp
GET BACK!!
SHOVE
WHOA...
WHOA!
WHOA!
WOBBLE
EEK?!
PLOOF
YOU'RE REALLY HINA, AREN'T YOU?
MREOW?
THAT'S DAN-GER-OUS, YOU KNOW.
What are you going to do if she turns into more of an idiot?
MITS--

NO...
DON'T COME OUT.
THIS OMINOUS PRESENCE IS...
MITSURU-CHAN?
NO. PLEASE.
SLIDE
THIS IS...
DON'T YOU DARE LAY A HAND ON EITHER OF THEM!!

AN EVIL SPIRIT!
TAMAKI-CHAN?!
......!!
THEY SAW!!

!!
MITSURU-CHAN!!
......
TAMAKI-CHAN.
YOU ALWAYS HAVE...
...YOUR JUZU, DON'T YOU?
gasp
THAT'S RIGHT.
TAMAKI-CHAN...
...HAS THE POWERS THAT THE CHILDREN OF THE OTOYA FAMILY INHERIT.

*Note: Juzu are Japanese prayer beads.

THE SHIELD OF PROTECTION, THE CREATION OF SPIRIT SERVANTS, THE SUMMONING OF PROTECTIVE SPELLS...
A SHUGOSHI MANIPULATES THOSE PROTECTIVE TECHNIQUES.
TAMAKI-CHAN IS THAT SOLE HEIR.
ASAHI-CHAN, YOU DON'T KNOW WHY SHUGOSHI EXIST, DO YOU?
EVIL SPIRITS ...?
IT'S TO EXORCISE EVIL SPIRITS.
THEY ARE THAT WHICH LATCH ON TO THE NEGATIVE FEELINGS IN YOUR HEART, LIKE SUSPICION AND HATRED...
...AND ACQUIRE STRANGE POWERS.
......!
YOU SAW ONE WITH YOUR OWN EYES DIDN'T YOU?
IT'S HARD TO TELL UNTIL YOU ACTUALLY CATCH THEM, THOUGH.

YOU'D ALREADY SENSED IT? MOTHER...
I AM A BRIDE OF THE OTOYA FAMILY, YOU KNOW. OF COURSE I HAVE A BIT OF POWER.
TAMAKI.
ONCE AN EVIL SPIRIT IS BORN, YOUR BLOOD ATTRACTS IT, YOU KNOW.
IT DOESN'T MATTER THAT YOU DON'T LIKE IT.
I DEFINITELY SAW IT.
THE OTHER SHADOW THAT APPEARED BEHIND MITSURU-CHAN.
THAT'S AN EVIL SPIRIT?
WHY?!
...I DON'T KNOW.
I DON'T KNOW, AND IT HAS NOTHING TO DO WITH ME.

I WON'T LET ANYONE GET CLOSE AGAIN.
NEVER AGAIN.
I CAN'T GO BACK.
DING
DONG
LUNCH! LUNCH! LUNCH-TIME!
ASAHI, YOU'RE GOING WITH OTOYA-KUN AGAIN, RIGHT?
YEP.
TORII-SAAN!!
DO YOU WANT TO JOIN US? IT MUST BE BORING BY YOURSELF ALL THE TIME.
BA-DUM
......!
DON'T BOTHER ME.

HEY...
YEP.
SHE'S COLD...
IT'S HARD TO GET CLOSE TO TORII-SAN, ISN'T IT...?
....
I DIDN'T WANT TO SEE HER LIKE THIS.
I DID WISH I COULD SEE HER, BUT...
THE PERSON I THOUGHT OF LIKE A MOTHER...

BACK THEN, THE ONLY REASON I SMILED WAS BECAUSE TA-MAKI-CHAN...
...AND MITSURU-CHAN WERE THERE.
THE THREE OF US ALWAYS PLAYED TO-GETHER...
...IN THE BAMBOO GROVE AT TAMAKI-CHAN'S HOUSE.
HINA.
COME HERE, HINA.
TAMAKI'S THE ONE YOU LOVE, RIGHT?
I LOVE YOU, MITSURU-CHAN.
I LOVE-LOVE TAMAKI-CHAN!
I LIKE-LOVE YOU, MITSURU-CHAN.
I CAN NEVER WIN WITH YOU.
AFTER ALL, YOU'RE REALLY A KID.

YOU'RE STILL THE SAME HINA, AREN'T YOU...
MITSU-RU...
YOU'RE THINKING ABOUT HER, AREN'T YOU?
BE-CAUSE...
MITSURU-CHAN'S THE ONE WHO'S SCARED, YOU KNOW.
SHE'S THE ONE WHO'S SCARED THE MOST.

TA--
......
TAMAKI-CHAN? IT'S NOT LIKE I WANT A KISS RIGHT NOW, BUT--OH, IT'S NOT LIKE I DON'T NEED ONE EITHER, BUT...
IT'S JUST A REFLEX, BECAUSE YOU PUT YOUR FACE CLOSE TO MINE.
Please stand by for a moment.
What the--?!
WHAT DID YOU SAY JUST NOW?! THEN ARE YOU SAYING THAT IF ANOTHER GIRL GETS THIS CLOSE TO YOU, YOU'D KISS HER, TOO?!
YOU'RE SAYING YOU WOULD EVEN IF IT WASN'T ME?! YOU'D DO IT TO SOME OTHER-- SOME OTHER GIRL ON THE STREET?!
...I GUESS YOU'RE A WOMAN, TOO.
YOU MEAN IT WOULD HAVE BEEN BETTER IF I WERE A BOY?!
How meeaan!

THERE'S NO REASON I COULDN'T USE IT NOW.
RIGHT NOW, IF I USE THE SPELL...
ぎゅっ
BUT...
...EVEN IF I COULD USE IT...
TAMAKI-CHAN?!
WHAT'S WRONG, TAMAKI-CHAN?!!
MITSURU?!
GET AHOLD OF YOURSELF.
PLEASE GET AHOLD OF YOURSELF.

HOW DID THIS...
WHAT'S WRONG, MANAGER?
MY LEG...
OW...
EVERY-ONE'S LEGS ARE--!!
ピーポーピーポー
REE-DOO REE-DOO REE-DOO
ザワ
ザワ
I have no clue what's going on.
They said something might be wrong with their bones...
It's creepy, isn't it? Weird.
ARE THEY GOING TO BE ALL RIGHT...
THE TRACK TEAM...?
......
I DON'T SENSE THAT PRESENCE...
SHE'S NOT HERE ANYMORE, IS SHE?
ガシャン
......!
YOU'RE WRONG.
I BELIEVE--
I BELIEVE IN MITSURU-CHAN!
PLEASE BELIEVE IN HER...

I UNDER-STAND.
YEAH...
MITSURU-CHAN.
giggle
......!
I FORGET MYSELF...
...MORE AND MORE...

I DON'T KNOW WHICH ONE IS ME...
...BUT...
I CAN'T ESCAPE.
MITSURU-CHAN?
......!
!
YOU'RE INVOLVED, AREN'T YOU?
IN ALL OF IT.

...THAT'S RIGHT.
AFTER ALL, I CAN'T SAY NO.
SINCE IT'S MY FAULT.
NONE OF THIS WOULD HAVE HAPPENED IF I DIDN'T EXIST.
WHY...?
I LOVE YOU.
I REALLY LOVE YOU, MITSURU-CHAN!
IS THAT SO?
I HATE YOU.

ASAHI!!
ASAHI!
YOU'RE WRONG.
THAT...
...MITSURU-CHAN WAS SMILING THE FIRST DAY SHE TRANSFERRED HERE!
SHE REMINISCED AND CALLED ME "HINA"!

I BELIEVE IN THAT MITSU-RU-CHAN!!
HA.
WHAT A HAPPY-GO-LUCKY KID.
I COMMEND YOU.
BUT IT'S NO GOOD.
I WON'T FORGIVE...
...THAT MITSURU...
...BECAUSE SHE TORTURED ME, WHO COULDN'T MOVE, THE WHOLE TIME.
......
WHO'RE YOU?
MITSURU SINNED.

WHEN I COULDN'T EVEN RAISE MY HAND AND WAS STUCK IN A SICKBED, SHE WAS RUNNING AROUND LAUGHING.
WHO DOES SHE THINK SHE OWES THAT TO?
IT'S ALL BECAUSE I GAVE HER EVERYTHING, ISN'T IT?
I AM MINORU.
MITSURU'S YOUNGER TWIN SISTER.

STOP!

This is the back of the book. You wouldn't want to spoil a great ending!

This book is printed "manga-style," in the authentic Japanese right-to-left format. Since none of the artwork has been flipped or altered, readers get to experience the story just as the creator intended. You've been asking for it, so TOKYOPOP® delivered: authentic, hot-off-the-press, and far more fun!

DIRECTIONS

If this is your first time reading manga-style, here's a quick guide to help you understand how it works.

It's easy... just start in the top right panel and follow the numbers. Have fun, and look for more 100% authentic manga from TOKYOPOP®!